EDUCATIONAL POLICY

Analysis, Structure, and Justification

Donna H. Kerr

University of Washington

David McKay Company, Inc.
New York

EDUCATIONAL POLICY: ANALYSIS,
STRUCTURE, AND JUSTIFICATION

Developmental Editor: Edward Artinian
Editorial and Design Supervisor: Nicole Benevento
Design: Pencils Portfolio
Production and Manufacturing Supervisor: Donald W. Strauss
Composition: Fuller Typesetting
Printing and Binding: Haddon Craftsmen

MANUFACTURED IN THE UNITED STATES OF AMERICA

Library of Congress Cataloging in Publication Data

Kerr, Donna H
  Educational policy.

  (Educational policy, planning, and theory)
  Includes bibliographical references and index.
  1. School management and organization.   I. Title.
LB2805.K44   379'.15   76-7459
ISBN 0-679-30307-3

PREFACE

THIS IS A PRACTICAL book, for it concerns what we actually do. It rests on the premise that the quality of our actions can be no greater than the quality of our understandings. More particularly, the quality of our making and implementing of educational policies depends, in large measure, upon the quality of our individual maps of the conceptual and normative terrain of educational policy.

But from the fact that this is a practical book, it does *not* follow that all persons will be able to put it to use merely by reading it in the way that one reads traffic signs or instructions on packages of freeze-dried foods. Those who come to questions of analysis and justification for the first time may find the exercise of supplying examples and illustrations from their own experiences to be most useful in integrating the considerations of this work into their actions. On the other hand, persons who are already comfortable with philosophical analysis and justification may best be served by a close criticism of the text. Still others might benefit more from some combination of these two types of readings.

To the extent to which this work succeeds in bringing "theoretical" questions to bear on educational practice, I must thank my educator-students in Alaska and at Teachers College, Columbia University, and the University of Washington.

They have consistently reminded me (1) that the way in which "abstract" considerations might be useful in making decisions is not necessarily obvious, (2) that even our most sophisticated understandings of educational policy making do not ensure enlightened action, and (3) that methods of philosophical analysis are powerful pedagogic tools. For their tough questioning and instructive insights, I especially wish to thank those students who have suffered my seminar on the study of educational policy.

I am notably indebted to three persons in particular for their careful criticism of the initial draft of this work. Robert E. Tostberg, my colleague at the University of Washington, has good-naturedly endured my recent preoccupation with this book. On reading the entire manuscript in chapter installments, he deftly took me to task in a number of most enjoyable sessions. Nuel D. Belnap of the Philosophy Department at the University of Pittsburgh provided detailed, thoughtful criticism of the first four chapters. And Jonas F. Soltis, my good friend and mentor when I was at Teachers College, Columbia University, responded to a draft of the first two chapters. As always, he offered constructive criticism and encouragement. I am confident that insofar as I have utilized the suggestions of Tostberg, Belnap, and Soltis, this work has been strengthened. Insofar as I did not, I travel at my own risk.

For her typing and retyping and fine editorial suggestions, I am grateful to Ilze Zigurs Powers.

And finally, my thanks to Stephen T. Kerr for introducing me to Professor Batty, who lends a bit of zaniness to chapter 3.

INTRODUCTION

AS AN INQUIRY THAT probes the elements of educational policy and policy making, this book is addressed to all educators, but not to all educators at all times. As an analytic inquiry, this book purports to provide guidance to educators but will admit to giving no advice. Further, this book is value neutral, yet it is written from a value-laden point of view. And finally, this book is designed to address a number of questions, though it is not intended to give the answers to any. It is through an unraveling of these seeming puzzles that I intend to acquaint the reader with the nature and purpose of the discussion that follows.

To begin, if a person were to pick up a book on, say, foreign policy and its making and if that person were one of the small circle of officials who are in a position to make foreign policy or if one were a "consulted expert," the obvious reason for reading that book would be because it addresses directly the questions of one's work. Others who might choose to read the book would do so either because they think that their indirect influence may affect foreign policy, because they are just curious, or perhaps because it is an "assigned text." One justification for any educator's reading *this* book would correctly be of the first type, the work-relevant justification. That is, every educator makes educational policy of some sort. The state superintendent, the classroom teacher, the national commissioner of education, the principal, and the librarian each make educational policy. And there are others who, though not professional educators, could also correctly invoke the work-relevant justification for reading this book, e.g., school board members and legislators. Further, because there are many educational policies that most educators, school board members, legislators, and others are in a position only to influence and not actually to make, they might appropriately use the influential-party justification for reading this book. The simply curious are justified in reading the book no matter what. (In the event that this discussion is read by persons for whom it is an assigned text, I hope that they will never read it for that reason alone.)

Clearly then, this is a book at least for all educators in that all educators make some educational policies and most educators work in the context of educational policies that they themselves can have an influential hand in shaping. But this is *not* a book for all educational policy makers at just *any* time. The person who is under pressure to make a particular policy decision usually wants advice that is specific to the policy under consideration. If any statement in this book can be "lifted out" and given a *direct* practical application to a policy decision, I am unaware of it. This is not, though, to say that the discussion has no practical application. Often a reflective pause, during which we analytically mull over the nature of the enterprise in which we are engaged, clarifies and gives fresh perspective. It is that clarification and freshness of view which may provide guidance. But, as noted, this book is virtually of no use and in fact might only provide one more frustrating experience for the person who is so preoccupied with a particular policy decision that only specific advice on "What should I do next?" seems relevant. My hunch is that this book would best be read during a "time out" from the pressures of immediate policy decisions, or at least it should not be read with the expectation that it will provide direct answers to particular policy problems. So much for the first two puzzles.

The third puzzle is my claim that this book is value neutral, yet written from a value-laden point of view. (Is there any other kind?) The tasks of this book are to analyze the concept of policy (chapter 1), to distinguish educational policy from just any policy (chapter 2), and to explore the conceptual and normative questions that are embedded in any case of educational policy making (chapters 3 through 5). Insofar as I carry out these tasks without prescribing a single educational policy, this undertaking is in one sense indeed value neutral. But the inquiry is heavily value laden in the sense that it presumes an overriding value of not only *rational*, but also *just* educational policy and policy making. At a time in which even organized movements extol the virtues of the irrational and when preoccupation with expediency too often reduces concerns with just action to lip service, some may think my presumed values to be presumptuous. I can only hope (and take to be the acid test of our educational policies) that to presume a moral point of view will not seem to presume too much.

And finally the last puzzle: while I have designed this book to address a number of questions, my intent is not to provide the answers. By "the answers," I mean answers that are in any serious sense final. For example, I address the conceptual question "What is a policy?," but I consider my answer to that question to be only tentative and improvable by further refinement or even by some basic revision. That is, this book focuses not on identifying *the* correct answer to each question (for those who seek such), but on developing answers that are offered as defensible on the basis of reasons which are open to the reader's scrutiny. I invite and encourage the reader to question and challenge with good reasons the analyses that constitute the discussion. Indeed, the point of my initiating this book is simply that: to provide an introduction to the philosophical analysis of educational policy and policy making. For the educator and other policy makers with little or no acquaintance with philosophical analysis, this book should serve as an introduction on how to motivate and think through fundamental conceptual and normative questions that are embedded in those policies which provide the context and often the content of educative efforts. To the beginning student of philosophy of education, it provides an analytic treatment of educational policy that suggests topics from political philosophy, social philosophy, decision theory, philosophy of law, and moral philosophy that might be productively pursued further in philosophy of education. For the philosopher who is interested in public policy, this book contributes to the literature an analysis of the neglected, yet central, concept of policy.

CONTENTS

ONE
THE NATURE
OF
POLICY

LANGUAGE FOR DESCRIBING POLICY

ON OBSERVING THE BEHAVIOR of bees, we might notice that sometimes bees do what appears to be a complicated, highly structured dance. We might further note that those bees that dance have just returned from finding food and, still further, that the dance serves to indicate to the other bees the general direction and approximate distance of the food from the location of the dance. It would seem appropriate to remark that this "dance" is regular, patterned behavior. It would, however, seem most inappropriate to say that the bees have a *policy* of communicating information on the location of food through the medium of a particular dance. That is, while we would readily attribute a communication function to the bees' behavior, we would not, except in a figurative sense, say that it is the bees' policy to communicate in that fashion.

In a similar vein, when talking about some things that human beings regularly do, we think it appropriate to use behavior language, but not policy language. For example, we may talk about how people typically behave when peeling onions. Most people cry, not because they choose to, but because they cannot help it. It's simply a reaction—part of "built in" behavior. It is not, then, because a bee is nonhuman that we find it odd to say that the bee has a policy. Rather, in both cases, policy language is inappropriate because neither the bee nor the human could do otherwise. Put in terms of the more general behavior-action distinction that has gained currency in philosophy of the social sciences, policy language is action language as opposed to behavior language.[1]

Especially in the talk of young children, examples abound of action language used to describe behavior that is not appropriately so describable. "Where does the sun go at night?" the child queries. Typically, the child who asks such a question is dissatisfied with an explanation in the appropriate *behavior*-of-celestial-bodies language. Instead, the child wishes to know exactly what it is that the sun decided to go off to do. The quest is for an *action*-language explanation, such as, "Oh, it goes to the other side of the world so

[1] For further discussion of the distinction between behavior and action descriptions, see Abraham Kaplan, *The Conduct of Inquiry* (Scranton, Pa.: Chandler, 1964), especially pp. 358–63. Kaplan casts the distinction in terms of "acts" and "actions." Thomas F. Green develops basically the same behavior-action distinction in a discussion of teaching, "Teaching, Acting and Behaving," *Harvard Educational Review* 35, no. 4 (November 1964): 507–24. For a discussion that extends the distinction beyond description to explanation, see Quentin Skinner, " 'Social Meaning' and the Explanation of Social Action," in *Philosophy, Politics and Society*, Fourth Series, ed. Peter Laslett, W. G. Runciman, and Quentin Skinner (Oxford: Basil Blackwell, 1972), pp. 136–57.

that it can make light for other people," as if the sun had a choice in the matter.

It is important to note, though, that while some regular "motions" that human beings go through, such as crying in response to the onion's spray, cannot appropriately be described in policy (action) language, a good many human doings can appropriately (depending on the intended use of the description) be described in action *as well as* behavior language. Take, for example, the case of talk that is carried on in classrooms. By describing what we see as a pattern of behavior, i.e., without regard to the intentions and purposes of students and teachers, we may learn that in classrooms with a "learning atmosphere," a pattern of communication exists that is distinct and different from classrooms in which the atmosphere seems hostile to learning. But if we wish to discuss, say, what teachers might take into account and attempt if they want to improve the learning atmosphere, we are talking not in behavior but in action terms.

Lest there be any doubt that policy language is action language, consider this. If a teacher-student exchange were describable as a particular communication pattern and if, at the same time, the teacher and student were not aware of their discussions forming any pattern at all, we would hardly think it correct to say that the teacher and students have a *policy* of so patterning their discussions. Other things that are done recurrently one might be aware of and still an ascription of a policy would not be warranted. Such might be the case with smoking. Smokers are surely aware of the fact that they smoke and perhaps that they smoke more frequently under particular conditions than others. Here we usually ascribe a habit, but not a policy, to the smoker. An individual might possibly have a policy of smoking on particular occasions for particular reasons, but typically one smokes from habit and not as a policy action. That is, if we are to talk of policy decisions, we must talk of someone's doing something with particular purposes in mind. Again, the particular "doing" *can* be described as either behavior or action, but if we wish to talk of the "doing" as policy, we must do so in action language, i.e., with reference to the doer's intentions, purposes, and related considerations.

Parenthetically it should be noted that policy doings are far from the only things that are appropriately described in action language. An American television program director decides to run a particular BBC series because it was highly acclaimed in England and thus might attract sponsors. I decide to climb Mount Rainier just so that I might have that experience. A parent decides to teach a child to fly a kite so that the child might have a diversion on windy days. In each case, someone does something for particular reasons or purposes; but in none of these cases would we say that the action counts as a policy. The running of the particular BBC series, the climbing of Mount Rainier, and the teaching of kite flying are things that one chooses to do for particular reasons, but not necessarily to do regularly for the achievement of further purposes. Put otherwise, a policy is describable by action language, but so are other intentional, purposive doings.

To recap, whatever else policies are, they are things that we choose and we could always decide otherwise; the doings that constitute the carrying out of a policy can be described as either behavior or as action, but if we are interested in the intents and purposes, then an action description is appropriate; and more than policy doings are describable in action language. Because one point of this book is to analyze policy in a way that might help us understand the elements of policy making, the formulating of a particular sort of plan of action to serve particular purposes, action language is appropriate to our task. We shall not, then, talk about policy with such phrases as "pattern of response," "structure of behavior," or "process output," as commonly policy has been treated in the literature of political science and the "policy sciences." Rather, we shall cast policy as one category of action which is planned and undertaken with particular purposes in mind.

WHAT IS A POLICY?

In the *Meno* when Socrates was asked, "Can virtue be taught?", he responded characteristically by saying that it depends on what one means by virtue. Meno then provided examples of virtuous behavior, for he thought that the examples themselves would tell what virtue is. Well, in a sense the examples are "telling," but (as Socrates pointed out) they do not by themselves give the answer. That is, though we cannot learn what a policy is merely by giving instances of policies, exemplars do provide a point from which to begin. By first providing examples of policies and then reviewing them in search of common features, we can initiate our analysis of the concept 'policy.'

As one example, consider the recently altered admissions policy of Princeton University. According to the policy announcement, when reviewing applications for admission to Princeton, the officers of the university will discriminate on the basis of merit and some other factors which were included in the earlier policy, but they will no longer discriminate on the basis of sex.[2] For a second example, think of the Department of Health, Education, and Welfare policy of withholding federal financial support from educational institutions that fail to meet HEW affirmative-action guidelines. Third, consider a particular school district's policy of deferring to the respective principals' judgments to decide whether any teacher should be granted tenure. For the

[2] See "The University," *Princeton Alumni Weekly* 74, no. 14 (5 February 1974): 6, 15.

fourth example, think of the myriad personal policies that one may have regarding his or her own education. More specifically, I ask the reader to imagine the following: person N has a policy of rising at four o'clock in the morning to read weighty philosophical texts, for N knows that the early morning hours provide the only time in which N can think clearly enough to comprehend them. While other examples will be introduced as needed, it is to these four policy exemplars that we refer throughout our analysis of 'policy.'

An initial review of these exemplars suggests that a policy consists of a plan of some agent or agency(A) to do something in particular (X). The officials of Princeton University (A) plan to use revised criteria (X). Officials of HEW (A) plan to withhold federal funds (X). The school board (A) plans to defer to the principals' judgments (X). And person N (A) plans to awaken at four o'clock to read (X). Now one might object that there are many policies "on the books" that have been ignored for years which do not have these features. Many are the policies according to which no one plans to do anything. Further, it could be said that these are indeed bona fide or official policies. Such are the contents of policy manuals that collect dust.

Let us imagine that the school board's policy of deferring to the principal's judgment in tenure decisions has acquired this "dusty" status. Let the scenario develop as follows: One day when the school board is making tenure decisions by a show of hands, a principal objects that the school board is not acting in accord with its tenure-decision policy, according to which the school board is to defer to the principal's judgment. The school board could make one of three responses: (1) it could produce an official policy record which shows the principal to be in error; (2) it could refer to the policy record which shows the principal to be correct and proceed to act in accord with the policy; or (3) it could say to the principal, "Yes, we know, but. . . ." If in fact the principal is in error, then the board is actually acting in accord with a plan for making tenure decisions and our analysis stands. If the board acknowledges that it is in error and alters its course of action to match the stated plan, then our analysis still seems correct, i.e., an agent and a plan to do something still appear to be features of policy. If the school board says, "Yes, but . . . ," that does not mean that there is no agent and plan of action. Rather, it suggests a violation of the policy—a violation by virtue of the fact that the agent fails to act in accord with the plan. Further, it might be noted that whether the policy's status is de jure or only de facto, to be a policy it must entail an agent's plan to do something in particular.

A second objection might be made. Consider the use of 'policy' in the neon sign of a used-car lot: "Honesty is our policy." And think of the teacher who asks the principal what his tenure policy is, to which the principal responds, "Excellence in teaching." Neither of these uses of the term suggests a plan to do anything in particular. The first makes a claim about the manner in which the used-car agency conducts its business. The second points to the purpose or goal of the principal's tenure policy. While acknowledging that the term 'policy' is indeed employed in these ways, we need not abandon our analysis to this point. Both uses logically derive from the broader plan-of-action use in our policy exemplars. Of the used-car dealer we could ask (and expect an affirmative answer), "Do you mean that whenever you are buying and selling automobiles, you try to be honest about their value?" This could be rewritten in our plan-of-action form: whenever assessing the value of automobiles for customers, the dealer plans to tell the customer what he actually believes to be the worth of the vehicles. If the dealer would not assent to the restatement under oath, as I suspect few dealers would, we would be correct in denying that he has any such policy and that his sign is at best a case of "harmless puffery" and at worst a downright lie. The case of the principal's tenure policy can be handled in a different manner, in that it refers only to the purpose or goal of the principal's policy. This being so, "excellence in teaching" should not be mistaken for the whole of the policy when it is but a part of the policy, namely the purpose.[3] That is, the principal's use of the term is truncated.

Truncated, but suggestive. Might it be that a policy is an agent's plan to do something in particular *for some purpose* and *necessarily* for some purpose? In each of our policy exemplars, there does seem to be a point to the agent's plan to do something in particular. At least one purpose of the new Princeton policy is to disallow sex discrimination in admissions procedures. The purported point of the HEW policy is to serve the goals of affirmative action. The purpose of the school board's policy would likely be to have tenure decisions made by persons who, in the school board's perception, know best whether a teacher should be granted tenure. The purpose of person *N*'s policy is to comprehend weighty philosophical texts.

Can we, though, conceive of a pointless or purposeless policy? That is, is a purpose a necessary feature of a policy? A caricature of an Alice-in-Wonderland organization comes to mind: everyone rushes about attending to the carrying out of "policies," but nobody remembers or can suggest the purpose of any of them. The tableau portrays the mindless following of now pointless, though perhaps "traditional"

---

[3] In the literature on educational policy in particular, this narrower use of 'policy' is frequently stipulated. For example, John Walton in his *Administration and Policy-making in Education* (Baltimore: Johns Hopkins Press, 1959), writes: "The phrase 'policy formation' we shall interpret to mean the setting up of purposes of an organization, making choices between conflicting purposes, and modifying established purposes" (pp. 44–45). When 'policy' is so used, the discussion of 'policy' must be limited to a consideration of purpose only.

procedures, and runs counter to the suggestion that policy seems to entail intelligent or purposive action. In the sense that we can conceive of the March Hare's being late when he's nothing to be late for, we can, I suppose, conceive of a pointless policy. But were the March Hare to make that limiting leap into the other world, we would surely counsel him on the conceptual requirements of 'being late.' Likewise, we would suggest that at least some point or purpose is necessary to this world's concept of policy.

At this point we can say, then, that a policy consists of a plan by some agent to do something for some purpose. While these features appear to be necessary, they are not sufficient to distinguish a policy from a planned itinerary or any other nonpolicy program of doings. For example, Jones (A) plans to go to Chicago next Tuesday and on to Munich on Friday (X) to deliver a series of lectures (the purpose, P). Yet we would be reluctant to say that Jones has a *policy* of going to Chicago and Munich as scheduled, even though Jones' travel plan has all the policy features that we have developed to this point. The crucial difference rests, I think, in the fact that while the travel plan is a single or "one shot" doing, a policy's doing is necessary iterative. Princeton admissions officers plan to apply the specified criteria *whenever* reviewing applications. HEW plans to withhold funds *whenever* affirmative-action guidelines are not followed to HEW's satisfaction. The school board plans to defer to the principals' respective judgments *whenever* tenure questions arise.

But could not we also say that Jones plans to go to Chicago *whenever* it is next Tuesday, and it just happens that next Tuesday comes only once? Clearly, it is not the word 'whenever' that makes the difference, but the agents' perceptions that the conditions under which they plan to do particular things will occur not once or twice, but an indefinite number of times. The use of "whenever" is simply one convenient way in which we might include the iterative element. It could be said, for example, that person N plans to rise to read philosophical texts *every morning* at four o'clock. With the understanding that it is the iterative feature and not the specific word 'whenever' that is crucial, let us supplement our policy constituents to read as follows: some agent (A) plans to do something in particular (X) whenever particular conditions (C) obtain, for some purpose (P).

While the addition of the iterative feature enables us to distinguish between policy and nonpolicy programs, our analysis is still not sufficiently rigorous to distinguish between general guidelines for action and policies. Consider the hypothetical case in which a school board (A) plans to defer to the principals' judgments (X) whenever a tenure decision needs to be made (C) for the purpose of having such decisions made by those who, at least in the board's perception, are most familiar with the teachers' competencies (P). Imagine, further, that at the same time the board has this plan in mind, the board members (A) stand ready to suspend the plan when it seems more convenient or advantageous to one or more of the board members to do so. That is, in this example the board does not view its plan as binding in all cases, which is the same as saying that it (A) views the plan as binding in no instance. We would, I think, be most hesitant to say that the board's plan constitutes a policy. The plan appears to be no more than a rough indication of how the board might handle most tenure decisions. If the board's claim to having a policy is to be considered bona fide, then the board must also intend to do the specified something (X) *whenever* the specified conditions (C) occur. In other words, by declaring a policy the agent obligates himself to act in accordance with an imperative which is of the form: whenever conditions C occur, do X. For the agent to do otherwise would be to violate the policy. For the agent to claim that he is under no obligation to do X whenever C, is to deny that he in fact has a policy.

Must the policy's imperative be a conditional one? Could the imperative be simply "do X" without "whenever conditions C occur?" One could argue that the necessary iterative element would not be lost as long as the agent is under obligation to act in accord with some imperative, for which an "open" or unconditional imperative would suffice. The result would be most odd. For example, officials of Princeton University would be obligated not to discriminate on the basis of sex *under any condition*. HEW would be committed to withholding funds *under all conditions*. And so on. To be obligated to do anything indiscriminately or unconditionally is to be obligated to do both far too much and too little, to do something too often and unmindfully so. So while the iterative feature would not be lost in allowing the imperative to be "open," the discriminating-action feature of policy would be sacrificed.

Sometimes one does encounter what on first blush would seem to be policies that contain a particular type of "open" imperative, i.e., a principle. Such is the case when a superintendent declares that his district has adopted a policy of equalizing the distribution of the district's educational resources among the students. In this case, what is to be done (X) is specified, though only in a general way (the policy's agents are to distribute educational resources equally among the district's students) and no conditions (C) are specified. Is this a policy? If the agent has not yet decided such issues as (1) what counts as an educational resource and (2) what might constitute an equal distribution of those resources, then it would seem odd to grant the superintendent that the district indeed has a policy. In such a case, i.e., when the decision regarding what is to be done has yet to be made, it would seem more correct to say that the district has adopted a *principle* for which a policy might be decided. If, on the other hand, the decisions regarding who (A) is to do what (X) whenever conditions (C) occur have already been made, then the imperative is in fact conditional and so needs no further comment, as our analysis holds.

To this point in our analysis, we can say that a policy exists when the following is satisfied: some agents or agency (A) must be obligated to act in accord with some conditional imperative, i.e., do something in particular (X) whenever specified conditions (C) occur, in order to achieve some purpose (P). While this description of policy is much richer and more precise than the initial suggestion of "someone plans to do something," much work remains to be done. In order to facilitate the further refinements and to keep the formulation from becoming too cumbersome, it will be helpful to restate the policy description as a set of conditions which must obtain if a plan for action is to count as a policy:

Condition 1. *Some agent or agency (A) must obligate itself to act in accord with some conditional imperative (I).*

Condition 2. *The conditional imperative (I) must be of the form, do something in particular (X), whenever specified conditions (C) occur.*

Condition 3. *The agent (A) undertakes the obligation (condition 1) in order to achieve some purpose (P).*

While we have advanced a considerable conceptual distance to reach this point, it is clear that we have still further to go when we notice that if the above are taken to be the only policy conditions, then promises may count as policies. Once again, let us turn to the case of an admissions policy. If a university has an admissions policy of admitting candidates who satisfy criteria *a, b,* and *c,* has the university, in effect, *promised* to admit all candidates who satisfy those criteria? That is, if the conditional imperative is, "Judge all applications on the basis of critieria *a, b,* and *c,* when reviewing applications for admission," and if the agent has obligated himself to act in accord with that imperative, is it not then the case that the agent has so promised? While the making of a promise and the adopting of a policy seem to share a number of features, they differ in three important ways.[4]

The first difference between policies and promises is already covered by the iterative feature of the conditional imperative. That is, "one shot" or limited-performance promises could not count as policies. If, for example, I were to promise to put a joke on page 50 of this book, I would be using the term 'policy' in a nonstandard way if I were to add that it is my policy to put a joke on page 50 of this book. It is those promises that announce an intention to do something every time particular conditions obtain, and to do so *indefinitely,* that present the interesting question. Are they different in any way from policies? From a comparison of these two kinds of promises, we uncover an important additional feature of policy. Namely, promises and policies are not "equally revisable." For example, if Jones *promises* to meet Smith every day at five o'clock to play handball, and if then after several days Jones rings up Smith to say that he will not be meeting Smith for handball anymore, no matter how convincing Jones' reasons or excuses, Jones has broken his promise. That is, if one revises a promise in any way, he has violated or broken it. But a policy can be revised without being violated or broken. Notice that when Princeton Uni-

---

[4] For one development of logical conditions for promising, see John R. Searle, *Speech Acts* (Cambridge: Cambridge University Press, 1969), chap. 3.

versity revised its admissions policy, it did not in so doing violate or breach its pre-revision policy. Care should be taken here to note what is *not* being claimed. I do not mean to suggest that policies cannot be broken. Clearly, not only is the violation of policies logically possible, but also evidently they can in practice be violated with ease. My point instead is that policies can (logically) be revised without being violated, whereas promises cannot.

In order to specify an additional policy condition that would distinguish policies from iterative-type promises, we need to specify how a policy might be revised without being violated. If a university were to announce one set of admissions criteria to its applicants and then to make its selections on the basis of a different set of criteria, we would say that the university had violated its admissions policy. The violations seem to occur when the agent says to some relevant persons that he will do X, but instead does X'.[5] Let us add a policy condition that concerns only those policies which have been announced:

Condition 4. *If the agent (A) does X' when conditions C' occur instead of X when conditions C occur, A has not violated his obligation to act in accordance with conditional imperative I, providing that A, prior to doing X', announced to the relevant persons his substitution of conditional imperative I' for I.*

[5] What, one might wonder, would we say if the university were to announce *no* criteria and then to switch its unannounced criteria immediately before or during the review of applications. Would such a change in criteria constitute a violation of the unannounced or hidden policy? The broader question asks under what conditions it might be said that a hidden policy has been violated— a question I do not treat here. For development of the notion 'fairly declared policy' as a policy announced to the relevant public, see Donna H. Kerr, "The Logic of 'Policy' and Successful Policies," *Policy Sciences* 7 (1976), in press.

REFINING THE POLICY CONDITIONS

In establishing the fourth policy condition, it could be said that we completed the initial, general analysis of the concept of policy, for with those conditions we can distinguish policy from related notions such as plan, program, program goal, principle, way of doing something, and promise. But while our analysis has been sufficiently rigorous to make those distinctions, our discussion has not been precise enough to lay the foundation that we shall need to distinguish educational policies from policies in general and to be of much help in identifying the fundamental issues of policy making. To the end of refining our analysis for these uses, let us address four questions which regard basic elements of the four policy conditions. In order of their discussion, the questions are as follows: (1) Who can be a policy's agent? (2) When does a doing (X) satisfy a conditional imperative (I)? (3) What can count as a policy's purpose? and (4) Who is a policy's public?

Who Can Be a Policy's Agent?

All of us at one time or another engage in the sometimes idle and sometimes constructive activity variously called daydreaming, thinking, reflecting, or the like. Frequently, thoughts focus on personal and social problems and goals. We try to devise means that could be used to solve the problems and achieve the goals. We think up Federal Reserve Board policies that could lessen economic problems, tax policies that would aid the development of public transportation, zoning policies that would improve the aesthetic quality of our urban environments, and a host of equally brilliantly conceived policies, including educational policies, that would enhance the quality of our lives. Also we concoct solutions to personal problems and methods for achieving personal goals. Leery of the effects of food additives on the human organism, one might decide to adopt a policy of preparing all foods from "scratch" and to use only pure ingredients. Wishing to build up stamina for mountain climbing, one might follow a policy of running fifty miles each week. With the goal of mastering ancient Greek, one might work out a policy of pouring over Greek texts on some regimen. And so forth.

Any persons who reflect on what is worth achieving have license to daydream their way to policies. But not just any person can adopt just any of these policies. Personal policies are "adoptable" only by the individual whose goals are to be served or whose problems are to be solved. In the matter of the adoption of my personal budgeting policies, logically only I am in a position to adopt them, to be their agent. You might have a policy of advising people, including me, what personal budgetary policies to adopt, but that clearly is not the same as being the agent of my budgetary policies. While only the given person logically can be the agent in a personal policy, the question of who can be a policy's agent poses a more complex task when we focus on social and otherwise public policies. As the daydreaming example suggests, almost anyone can have an idea about what those policies should be, but far from just anyone can be their agent. I might write a letter to the Federal Reserve Board to recommend that they adopt a particular policy, but I cannot adopt that policy for them, as I could in the case of my personal budgetary policy. Especially since policies of the nonpersonal type would seem to concern educational policy makers most, the question of who can be their agents needs attention.

Initially, it may be helpful to pose a prior question: can a policy have more than one type of agent? Recall the case of the revised admissions policy at Princeton University.

Earlier we identified the agents as the admissions officers, i.e., those employees of the university who are responsible for making the decision on each application. But the admissions officers did not decide what the admissions policy should be. That decision was made by the Board of Trustees. Further, it may not be the admissions officers who actually apply the criteria to the bulk of applications. Administrative assistants may well attend to that. To demand who is the "real" agent seems misguided. They are all agents of the policy in some sense. In the same way, to ask which is the main agent of the policy might misdirect us, for without either the admissions officers or the administrative assistants, the policy could not actually be put into effect.

It seems more productive to distinguish two types of agents: *authorizing agents* (A_a), such as the Board of Trustees, and *implementing agents* (A_i), such as the admissions officers and their deputies, the administrative assistants. Not only can a policy have more than one type of agent, but also nonpersonal policies commonly do. The question of who can be a policy's agent now has two readings: First, who can be a policy's authorizing agent (A_a)? Second, who can be its implementing agent (A_i)? The second does not appear to be problematic in this context, though of course it might be in a theory of organizations. Anyone who is acting for or on behalf of the authorizing agent could be an implementing agent (A_i). Typically, such would be true only of persons who hold positions on the organizational chart under that of the authorizing agent, though that need not necessarily be so. The first of the questions presents far the more interesting issue: who can be a policy's authorizing agent (A_a)?

At first glance, it would seem that who can be a policy's authorizing agent might also be decidable by appealing to some organizational chart and set of job descriptions. The line of reasoning of this view is: (1) most nonpersonal policies are made within the structures of public institutions and organizations; (2) public institutions and other organizations function according to well-defined tasks and assignments; (3) policies are made as one means of carrying out organizational tasks; (4) therefore, if a policy is made within the structure of a public institution or other organization, who can be the authorizing agent of any policy may be determined by checking who has been assigned the task that the policy in question addresses. Take, for example, the local Ajax Rent-a-Car Company. The personnel manager and nobody else can (*read:* is designated by the organizational rules to . . .) determine personnel policies; the business manager and nobody else can (again *read:* is designated by the organizational rules to . . .) determine business policies. The matter is cut-and-dried. Or is it? Consider an eighteenth-century ship's captain. 'Tis he who decides policy for the running of the ship until, of course, the sailors mutiny and ignore the captain's wishes. One sailor from the ranks "takes charge" and, quite aside from prescriptions of the organizational chart, begins to make policy. And if he does in fact make policy, are not we obliged to admit that he logically *can* make policy?

The question to be answered is, when does someone have *authority* to make a policy? Our first answer (the Ajax Rent-a-Car case) was, whenever that person has de jure authority. Our second answer (the mutinous sailor's case) was, whenever that person has de facto authority.[6] There are, then, not one but two questions to be answered: First, who can according to the rules (laws, customs, traditions, etc.) be a policy's authorizing agent? Second, who can by virtue of effective influence (persuasion, charisma, and

[6] For an excellent brief guide to further discussions of de jure and de facto authority, see Stanley I. Benn, "Authority," in *The Encyclopedia of Philosophy,* ed. Paul Edwards (New York: Macmillan & Free Press, 1967).

maybe brute force) be a policy's authorizing agent? [7] The
first presents no difficulty, for we have only to appeal to the
relevant rules. The second requires closer attention. When,
we must decide, is a person's effective influence such that
he can in fact make a particular policy?

Recall that when one has a policy he undertakes to do
X whenever conditions C obtain. Might it be, then, that one
may be said to have effective influence when he can in fact
himself do X or have X done when conditions C occur? In
the case of the HEW policy, we would say that whoever does
not possess de jure authority and yet acts in the place of the
HEW officials (who have de jure authority) would have de
facto authority if they could indeed succeed in withholding
federal funds from educational institutions (X) whenever
those institutions fail to follow HEW affirmative-action
guidelines. If for any reason the unofficial agents were unable to withhold the funds under those conditions, whether
because of ignorance about how to cut off the funds or lack
of access to the "supply line," we would say that they are not
in fact the policy's de facto authorizing agents.

While de jure and de facto authority are distinct types
of authority, they are not in practice mutually exclusive. In
a random sample of authorizing agents of policies, some
agents would possess de jure authority only, others de facto
authority, still others both types. In times of insurrection,
rioting, and revolution—events not unknown even in educational institutions—the administrators who are the de jure

---

[7] My allowing brute force to count as authority qua effective
influence is at seeming odds with R. S. Peters' discussion of 'authority' in his *Authority, Responsibility and Education* (3rd ed.;
London: George Allen & Unwin, 1973). To Peters, "the concept of
'authority' is necessary to pinpoint ways in which behavior is regulated *without* recourse to power—to force, propaganda, and threats"
(p. 19). The point here is not to take issue with Peters' analysis,
but to note that if a person has no de facto authority to make a
policy, then force, whether classified as simply power or authority,
can put that person in a position to be the agent of that policy.

authorizing agents of a wide range of policies may be rendered impotent for lack or loss of de facto authority. The leader of the insurrection may enjoy de facto authority, but not de jure authority, though the point of the insurrection may well be to change the rules in order to gain de jure authority. But in other cases—and indeed in most examples of policies developed within a generally accepted set of laws, customs, or traditions—the authorizing agent of any policy possesses both types of authority, at least to some extent.

I submit that the primary concern of the policy maker who wishes to make effective policies is to have de facto authority. While de jure authority by itself is little better than are royal titles to the court of a deposed monarchy, de facto authority (with or without de jure authority) enables the agent to establish policies. One wonders, then, over what or whom or in whose view a person must have authority qua effective influence in order to be a policy's authorizing agent? The obvious but uninstructive and potentially misleading answer is that he must have effective influence over all the people involved. It is obvious because it is tautological, uninstructive because such is the nature of tautology, and potentially misleading because it wrongly suggests that everyone who is in any way affected by the policy must somehow "go along" with it.

Consider the case of a store manager (A_a) who has a policy of having his security guards (A_i) apprehend persons whenever they are seen leaving the store with goods for which they have not paid. It is not the shoplifter but the security guard (A_i) who must recognize the store manager as the authorizing agent of any such policy. This is to say, an authorizing agent must have authority (effective influence), over the implementing agent, and *not* over the shoplifter. The goal of the policy may be to alter the behavior of the would-be thief and to recover stolen goods, but it is neither the thief's behavior nor the goods over which the store manager must have authority in order to qualify as the policy's authorizing agent. In the case of a policy in which the authorizing agent and the implementing agent are the same person, such as is always the case with personal policies and often the case in policies of nonbureaucratized institutions, the agent need only be able to get himself to do X whenever conditions C occur. At first, one is tempted to believe that in those cases in which one person serves as both types of agent, the problem of authority in policy making disappears, for the agent need have authority over no other person. But a second thought reminds us that strength of resolve, tenacity, stick-to-it-ness—otherwise called self-control—determines whether a person does in fact have the authority over self that is required if he is to authorize the implementation of his own policies.

A decision on whether the above-mentioned conditional imperative is an effective tool in altering the behavior of the would-be thief and in recovering the goods is a separate matter and should not be confused with the issue of the policy's authorizing agent. In other words, the questions of whether a policy is effective and whether someone can be a policy's authorizing agent should be kept distinct, lest we deny the logical possibility (and not uncommon occurrence) of one's being in a position to be the authorizing agent of an ineffective policy.

The only way, then, in which the adopting of a policy may correctly be conceived as the giving of a command or exercising of authority over someone is with reference to the directive that the authorizing agent (A_a) gives to the thus-named implementing agent (A_i).[8] The authorizing agent, contrary to what might intuitively seem to be the case, does not command the persons (other than the implementing

---

[8] For a closer discussion of the exercise of authority, see C. W. Cassinelli, *Free Activities and Interpersonal Relations* (The Hague: Martinus Nijhoff, 1966), pp. 59–64.

agents) who are in some way to be affected by the policy (i.e., the relevant public) to do anything. Rather he decides upon conditions C under which he or some other person as implementing agent will take particular actions. In those instances in which we observe that the policy's authorizing agent does attempt to command the relevant public to do particular things, we are correct in describing him as either preaching or attempting to coopt that public into serving as implementing agents.

When, for example, a university adopts a policy regarding degree requirements, it directs (exercises authority over) certain officials of the university to grant a candidate a degree (X) whenever that candidate has satisfied specified requirements (C). The university does not direct the candidate to earn the degree, i.e., to make the conditions obtain under which the officials have been directed to grant a degree. In announcing the policy to the relevant public of aspirants and potential aspirants for the degree, the university informs those persons of what actions under what conditions the university (A_a) obligates itself to direct its admissions officers (A_i) to take. Thus, acting as authorizing agents of its own policies, a university logically cannot command or "exercise authority over" anyone other than its own implementing agents. Let us, then, tighten the first policy condition to read:

> *Some authorizing agent (A_a) obligates itself to direct some implementing agent (A_i) to act in accord with a specified conditional imperative.*

When Does a Doing Satisfy a Conditional Imperative?

Frequently disputes arise over whether the implementing agent's "doings" satisfy the policy's conditional imperative. In order to clarify when, according to the logic of policy, a doing may correctly be said to satisfy a conditional imperative, consider the following case of a hypothetical faculty-promotion policy of some college. According to this hypothetical policy, whenever an assistant professor applies for promotion, first the faculty members of higher rank (A_i-1) shall individually evaluate the application on the basis of specified criteria (e.g., excellence in scholarship, teaching, and service); and if more than x percent of the voting faculty members deem that the application satisfies the criteria, then the dean of the college (A_i-2) shall recommend to the president of the university that the applicant be promoted. For purposes of this discussion, we may limit our consideration to the "doing" of the first set of implementing agents (A_i-1), the faculty members. In this example the question is, when logically does a faculty member's doing satisfy the conditional imperative?

We are not here concerned with the practical problem of how to determine in a particular case whether faculty members did in fact arrive at their voting decision in the manner the policy specifies. Such is the problem that one would face when attempting to decide whether a particular policy has been breached. The matter that concerns us here is, to just what "doing" does a policy obligate the agent? In our hypothetical example, let us say that some faculty members believe that the policy obligates them only to cast a yes or no vote, i.e., to evaluate the application but not on any particular bases. Now the rest of the faculty members believe that the policy obligates them to cast a yes or no vote on the basis of specified criteria. It would appear that clearly only the latter are correct in their belief, yet the "any-bases" evaluators argue that they too are correct. Their line of reasoning is as follows: (1) how members think through the application of criteria varies from member to member; (2) thus, members who apply the specified criteria do not always agree; (3) therefore, the policy does not in effect really require that the specified criteria be used. Here the "any-bases" evaluators seem to confound the effect of the policy and the obligation of policy agents. As agents, they cannot have it both ways. Either their doings satisfy the conditions for X-ing (here, evaluating applications on the basis of specified criteria) or they have violated the policy. That is, a doing satisfies the conditional imperative only if that doing fulfills the conditions for the specified X-ing.

Since what doings should count as satisfying the policy's imperative is too commonly misunderstood, the point merits a restatement, this time without the flesh that fully developed examples provide. The argument that constitutes the misunderstanding goes as follows: (1) according to the policy, A_i is supposed to X whenever conditions C occur; (2) we all know that there are lots of things that one could do that would count as X-ing; (3) because there are lots of different things (maybe even infinite in number) that one could do that would count as X-ing, anything counts as X-ing. If persons could do things with no more variation than a computer does, i.e., if there were only one or a very few detailed activities that could count as X-ing, this problem would not arise. But clearly no two human doings, even when both count as X-ing, are the same in all describable detail.

Yet we are not warranted in taking the jump of step 3 to say that therefore just about anything counts as X-ing. Many things that one could do would count as teaching or gardening, for example, but *not just anything* counts. The mistake of step 3 seems to derive from the incorrect assumption that what counts as X-ing must be specifiable by reference to some delineated class of doings that always count as X-ing, where no other doings can count, if the policy's imperative is "really" to obligate the agent to doing literally what the imperative specifies. Typically, the person who makes the step-3 mistake claims that if a policy doesn't "say exactly" what is supposed to be done, then it doesn't say anything. The mistake would not be made if the implementing agent were to recognize (1) that the X that a policy prescribes may be a polymorphous activity and (2) that when the X is a polymorphous activity, the agent is obliged to do *something that counts as some specified X-ing* whenever conditions C occur.[9]

To this point, we can refine our statement of the second policy condition to read:

The conditional imperative must be of the form, do something that counts as some specified X-ing, whenever specified conditions C occur.

A second refinement of this condition may serve to avert another typical confusion over what a policy requires of an agent—a refinement that regards the second part of the conditional imperative, the conditions C. We have noted that an agent's doing satisfies a conditional imperative if the agent's doing counts as X-ing whenever specified conditions occur. But agents sometimes imagine an additional qualifier, "except where 'discretion' suggests otherwise or when there are extenuating circumstances." To exemplify such a mistaken reading of the conditional clause, consider that case of a college admissions officer's admitting an applicant who did not meet the criteria as specified in the admissions policy. When queried, the officer acknowledges that the applicant did not satisfy the criteria and adds that he "felt sorry" for the applicant and so admitted her anyhow. Further, the officer claims to have acted in accord with the

---

[9] For a more thorough motivation of the need to talk of "condition for X-ing" rather than simply to specify genus activities for which any properly related species would count, see Gilbert Ryle's discussion of polymorphous concepts in "Thinking and Language," *Proceedings of the Aristotelian Society*, Supplement 25 (1951): 65–82.

policy; he's just "using his discretion" or "there were extenuating circumstances." And he might not have admitted someone who did satisfy the criteria for the same reasons. In effect, the admissions officer is claiming that whether or not specified conditions C occur, if unspecified extenuating conditions E occur, then whether he does or does not do X, he still may be said to be acting in accord with the policy.

Clearly, such a "discretionary" blank check negates the logic that constitutes a policy. This is not, of course, to claim that policies logically cannot be written to include clauses that specify discretionary bounds. The point is, if the discretion factor is not built into the policy's conditions and if that discretion is not delimited, then such discretion logically cannot be exercised without violating the policy. To block explicitly the claim that the exercise of nonspecified discretion is not a policy violation, let the second policy condition read:

> *The conditional imperative must be of the form, do something that counts as some specified X-ing whenever,* without exception, *specified conditions C occur.*

This is not to say that policies should never be violated. The point is that we should recognize when we are violating them.

To avert a potential misunderstanding about what is being claimed here regarding the use of discretion and policies, a distinction needs to be made between the use of discretion that constitutes a breach of policy (as discussed above) and the use of discretion that may well enhance the proper implementation of a policy. When, for example, an implementing agent must decide whether conditions C do in fact obtain and determine what might be a good way to do X, it would clearly not constitute a prima facie violation of the given policy if the agent were to exercise discretion qua use his best judgment. The exercise of discretion that constitutes a policy violation is one that supports an action which is at variance with the action that the policy specifies. On the other hand, the exercise of discretion that consists in using one's best judgment to determine whether in fact the policy conditions obtain and what the policy specifies is to be done is not a violation and, indeed, would seem to promote proper implementation of the policy.

What Can Count as a Policy's Purpose?

Having refined the first two policy conditions, we now turn to the third which, in light of the above revision regarding the agent, may initially be rewritten as: the authorizing agent (A_a) undertakes the condition-1 obligation in order to achieve some purpose. From the outset, it should be perspicuous that almost anything the authorizing agent wishes can count as a policy's purpose. If I have a policy of running at least ten miles each day, my purpose could be any of a very large number of things, e.g., to keep my stamina up for my yearly mountain-climbing expeditions, to see if I can run ten miles a day for as long as I live, to impress my constituency with my commitment to physical fitness, to increase my income by testing running shoes for sporting goods companies, to make sure that each day I "get away" from the strains of my professional life, or for any number of other purposes or some combination of such purposes. While it seems obvious enough that a policy's purpose depends upon what the authorizing agent has in mind and that in any given case that purpose could reasonably be any of a large number of purposes, it evidently is not obvious that a policy might have multiple purposes. All too commonly, critics of policies are quick to suggest policy revisions designed with but one purpose of the policy in mind. Such is often the case with personal policies, the purposes of which we somehow never manage to put in writing. It is only well after our policy revision, when we observe that "things are going wrong," that the forgotten purposes for which we designed the first policy return to mind.

A perhaps conceptually less obvious point is that not all purposes are achievable, yet they can count as a policy's purpose. Further, other purposes are such that in their achievement, the policy is logically dissolved. Still other purposes are such that if they are not achieved repeatedly, then the policy purpose is not being served. And yet the achievement of still other purposes counts only as a partial achievement of the policy's purpose. To confound these four categories of purposes is to risk misunderstanding what should be expected of any given policy. Bearing in mind that any policy may have multiple purposes and that those purposes may belong to different categories, we see that the point here is *not* that any given policy has purposes that fall within but one of the four categories, though that may be the case. Rather, only if we know the nature of each of the policy's purposes can we know when a policy is serving its purposes. Let us consider the four categories of purposes in the order mentioned and label them, respectively, *unachievable* purposes, *once-achievable* purposes, *repeatedly achievable* purposes, and *embedded* purposes.

Perhaps the most famous of *unachievable* purposes is the perfection of the mouse trap. We can imagine that some inveterate inventor might adopt a policy of laboring in his shop every evening for the purpose of perfecting the mouse trap. This category of purpose does not want for more "serious" examples. Many a Soviet education policy has been designed for the purpose of developing persons in the image of the "New Soviet Man," an image of perfection. Many a ballet instructor has pedagogic policies, the purpose of which is to get his students to perform in perfect form. Many a personal policy has been undertaken in pursuit of happiness or some other "perfect" state. Those purposes which refer to perfect or ideal states of affairs are, by definition, not achievable. One is reminded of Zeno's paradoxes. No matter how fine the state of affairs one achieves with the policy, there is always a finer one on the horizon. Note that the unachievability of this sort of purpose does not necessarily reflect foolishness of purpose. For example, the educator who adopts a policy, the purpose of which is to develop rationally critical minds, would not be thought a fool for *aiming* at the development of *perfectly* rationally critical minds. He would be considered a fool only if he thought such a state of affairs achievable. The measure of success of a logically unachievable policy is not whether the ideal state of affairs is effected but whether it brings about progressively "more perfect" states of affairs. The inventor's policy is, then, serving its purpose if by following it the inventor is in fact developing better and better mouse traps. In general terms, an unachievable-purpose policy is serving its purpose if it is effecting states of affairs that progressively resemble more closely the ideal state of affairs to which the purpose refers.

The second category is that of *once-achievable* purposes. A parent may adopt particular pedagogic policies for the purpose of getting his child to learn to do particular computations, to pass some standardized examination, or to learn to swim well enough to earn some lifesaving certificate. NASA officials may adopt a number of research coordination policies, the purpose of which is to develop technology that would allow a spaceship to lift off and land at any airport equipped to handle 747s. In these cases the policy's purpose is logically achievable and achievable only once. Further, once the purpose of the policy has been achieved, that purpose can no longer count as the agent's purpose for acting in accord with the conditional imperative. If one wanted to decide whether a policy with a once-achievable purpose were serving its purpose, he would have either (1) to estimate whether the policy was effecting states of affairs that would make progressively more likely the effecting of the state of affairs to which the purpose refers or (2) to "wait and see," in which case he could determine only if the policy's purpose had been achieved and not whether it was, say, "on the verge" of being achieved.

In sharp contrast to once-achievable purposes are *repeatedly achievable* purposes. Such is the nature of maintenance policies. Take as an example a janitorial policy, the purpose of which is to keep some building clean. In order for the purpose to be served, the building might have to be scrubbed from top to bottom every night. In policies with such maintenance purposes, some state of affairs (here, a clean building) must be achieved repeatedly for the purpose of the policy to be served. Such policy purposes are not limited to strictly routine tasks. A physician might have (the patient hopes this to be the case) a policy of keeping abreast of the latest research as might bear on the advisability of various treatments. Again, the purpose is such that there is no point at which the physician could say that the policy's purpose has been finally achieved, except perhaps in some figurative sense. Time after time, the physician's actions must bring about a state of affairs in which the physician may correctly be said to be "up on" the relevant findings, if that policy is to count as serving its purpose. Whatever the example, this sort of purpose is served if and only if the agent's acting in accord with the conditional imperative *repeatedly* brings about the specified state of affairs. How often counts as "repeatedly" would vary from case to case.

The fourth category of purposes is not, strictly speaking, parallel to the other three. That is, purposes that fall in the other three categories may also be placed in the fourth category, the category of *embedded* purposes. Failure to recognize and examine purposes as embedded purposes allows us to adopt unknowingly policies that work at cross purposes or to hold purposes which, contrary to what we may believe, do not serve our "real" or broader purposes. In both personal and social policies we typically embed some purposes in others; thus, a good many policies that concern us would count as embedded policies. One adopts a policy of running ten miles a day to build stamina for a yearly mountain-climbing expedition in order to build a public image that will consistently attract votes in order to hold on to a Senate seat in order to develop legislation to protect the environment in order to. . . . In such a string of policies which are linked by their purposes, if one does not keep sight of the latter, "outer" policy purposes, the former, "inner" purposes may be achieved in such a way as to hinder the "outer" purposes. For example, if the particular policy of climbing a mountain every year were carried out in such a way as to destroy high-altitude ecosystems, the purpose of collecting sufficient votes to maintain the Senate seat may still be served, but the purpose of developing legislation to protect the environment may well be hindered.

The logical point is this: if the purpose of a policy is embedded in other purposes, then an agent's acting in accord with a conditional imperative may both serve and not serve the policy's purpose. That is, it may serve the immediate purpose (p) of the policy, but not the more encompassing purpose (P) for which a policy with the immediate purpose (p) was designed. In like manner, it may serve some policy's broader purpose (P), but not the more narrow purpose (p). Such might be the case if the climbing expeditions did not build the image to collect necessary votes and so the senator lost his seat, but at the same time the mountain climbing did draw the public's attention to the environment in such a way that the public then exerted pressure on the Congress to pass legislation to protect the environment.

In discussion of the four categories of purposes that policies might have, purposes were always treated as states of affairs to be brought about, or at least to be pursued, when the state of affairs was some ideal state. And indeed, a policy that has no purpose which refers to some state of affairs seems inconceivable. Yet, we can think of purposes that do not refer to states of affairs, e.g., the purpose of acting justly. That is, while every policy logically must have a purpose that refers to some state of affairs, it may have other purposes that do not refer to states of affairs. If one wants to bring about a state of affairs in which he has a ticket to Oslo in his pocket, he will have to choose means for achieving that state of affairs. There is a second, *non*-state-of-affairs purpose he may have in mind. He may wish to obtain the ticket in a legal or moral way, for example. His second purpose, to act morally, is not a type of purpose that can serve as the policy's sole purpose. To act legally or morally, one must do so in the carrying out of other purposes which must refer to states of affairs. But to the contrary, one *can* carry out state-of-affairs purposes without having in mind purposes that restrict the manner. That to which such purposes refer has been variously labeled "principles of procedures," [10] "planning principles," [11] and in moral philoso-

---

[10] R. S. Peters, "Must an Educator Have an Aim," in his *Authority, Responsibility and Education*, pp. 122–31. While at the end of this paper, Peters treats "principles of procedure" as restrictive principles (p. 131), earlier he confounds them with unachievable state-of-affairs purposes, and so mistakenly regards the latter as improper goals of education (p. 124).

[11] Abraham Kaplan, "On the Strategy of Social Planning," *Policy Sciences* 4, no. 1 (March 1973): 41–61. In Kaplan's description planning principles "do not determine the ends of . . . action in terms of which a planner can formulate goals and objectives. Rather, they set limits to such ends and to the programs by which ends may be realized" (p. 53).

phy, "deontological rules." [12] To remind us of their restrictive quality and the fact that they cannot stand alone as a policy's purpose, we shall call them *restrictive purposes.*

Because purposes of the restrictive type are not things one "achieves" but are fulfilled by following rules in attempting to achieve the state-of-affairs purposes, the third policy condition needs to be refined to distinguish between the two:

> *The authorizing agent (A_a) undertakes the condition-1 obligation for the purpose of effecting some specified state of affairs (S) and to do so without violating any restrictive rules (R) by which (A_a) would claim to abide.*

From the above discussion of S-type purposes, it should be borne in mind that "effecting some specified state of affairs (S)" means either to effect an approximation that is as close as possible to ideal S, to achieve S but once, or to repeatedly achieve some S, depending on the type of S-purpose. Further, any policy may specify more than one state of affairs, and any S-type purposes of one policy may be embedded in those of other plans of action.

Who Is a Policy's Public?

Recall that according to the fourth policy condition, a policy may be revised without being violated if the revision is announced to the relevant public. This condition tells us

[12] While ethical theories can be divided into exclusive classes of deontological theories and teleological theories (see C. D. Broad, *Five Types of Ethical Theories* [London: Routledge & Kegan Paul, 1930], esp. pp. 206–8), any plan of action (including policy) can be chosen on both deontological and teleological grounds. Those who would insist that deontological rules be brought to bear in every policy decision would *not* argue that one should not act teleologically, i.e., with ends-in-view. Rather, they would argue that deontological rules are of higher lexical order than rules which specify states of affairs to be achieved.

two things. As noted earlier, it distinguishes policies from promises. Second, it suggests that one must use a notion of "relevant persons" if one is adequately to explicate the concept of policy. Who are, one wonders, the "relevant persons"? In other words, what distinguishes the relevant persons of a policy from just any persons? Or, more simply, who is a policy's public? While at this point the question arises from an interest in clarifying the logical elements of policy, a number of practical issues hinge on our response, e.g., in a given case, has the policy been violated; was the policy fairly declared; is the policy maker considering the views of those he should in the manner he should?

Initially, let us consider the obvious proposal that a policy's public consists of all persons who are in any way affected by the policy. According to this criterion, persons who wish to apply to a university would qualify as at least part of the public of a university's admissions policy, for they are clearly affected by the policy. But are all applicants "affected"? Or are the only ones really affected those who, because of the stringent requirements, are denied admission? And might not the policy affect many other persons whom we would be reluctant to categorize as part of the policy's public?

Consider, for example, an applicant's great-uncle who is profoundly disappointed because his nephew was not admitted to the university. The great-uncle would clearly qualify as one who was affected by the admissions policy, yet intuitively it does not seem that the great-uncle should count as part of the relevant public. Or, should one think the uncle a part of the public, we might extend the point two more "ripples" outward. Imagine that the great-uncle, on learning that his nephew was not admitted to the university, sends that sum of money which would have gone to pay for the lad's university years to a relief organization which, in turn, uses the sum to transport medical supplies to a typhoon-devastated coast of India. Would not we agree that the person whose life was saved thanks to the typhoid shot was surely affected by the admissions policy, even if only indirectly so? Yet, to say that the fortunate Indian is a part of the public of the admissions policy seems absurd.

Might it be, then, that only those persons who are affected by the "first ripple" constitute the relevant public? Take the case of the Pentagon's policy of granting contracts to the "most attractive" offer. More than once, this policy has led to a job boom in some city T. In order to cope with the additional population, the city has had to increase public services and facilities. Then, when the fighter planes (or whatever the contract calls for) have been built, the subsequent contract is granted to a different company in another city. At that point, the population of city T drops, leaving the remaining taxpayers with the burden of the additional public facilities to maintain. Though the citizens of T are several ripples removed from the policy, it still seems that they should be considered a part of the relevant public. Thus, it appears that the proposed criterion of "whoever is affected" allows persons who do not reasonably seem to count as part of the relevant public (e.g., the fortunate Indian). Further, by narrowing the criterion to exclude all persons beyond those who are most immediately affected (the first ripple), we eliminate some who it seems ought to be included (e.g., the citizens of T).

So we gain no clarification by the suggestion that those persons who are in some way affected by the agent's doing the X that the policy specifies constitute the policy's public. Nevertheless, might it be the case that those persons who can bring about the conditions C, under which the agent is obligated to do X, constitute the public? According to this suggestion, in the case of the admissions policy, the public would consist of those persons who might consider applying for admission to the university—an action which occasions an application review (C) which means that the admissions officers are obligated to apply the specified criteria, i.e., to do X. In the case of the Pentagon's contract policy, the public would be constituted by the various directors of companies who might consider trying to submit the "most attractive" offer. The suggestion seems correct. Any person who is in a position to decide whether to bring about the conditions to occasion the specified policy action does appear to count as a part of the relevant public. But clearly the set of persons who are in such a position does not include all persons that we might consider part of the relevant public. There are others. For example, the taxpayers of T are not in a position to decide whether to bring about the conditions as specified in the Pentagon's policy, yet the taxpayers do seem to be part of the relevant public.

Having established one subset, we face the task of identifying the balance of the set of the relevant public. Recall that the typhoon victim did not seem to be part of the public of the university admissions policy, yet the taxpayer, who was as many "ripples" removed, did seem to qualify in the case of the Pentagon policy. Why one and not the other? The crucial difference, I submit, is to be found in the system or systems of rules within which the policy is made. Policy decisions of U.S. governmental agencies are made within the context of the U.S. political system, which is defined by rules which, among other things, specify (1) that the militia serves at the pleasure of civil government, and (2) that citizens are constitutionally empowered to determine, within a system of specified rules, the actions of their government. It is, then, the taxpayer's right as citizen that his view be taken into consideration as constitutionally defined. In more general terms, those persons whose views are to be given due-by-law consideration in the making of a policy count as at least part of the relevant public of that policy. In other words, a relevant public can, at least in part, be legally defined. Or, it could be defined by a theory of justice (or some other theory of right), under which the relevant public would consist at least of those persons whose views would have to be taken into account if the policy decision is to count as a just decision. So then, the second subset of the relevant public must be specified with reference to some political system or moral order, or both. To be sure, those who under one system or order would constitute the relevant public may not do so under another. Under Nazi policies, Jews were merely objects and not part of the relevant public as defined by the Nazi government; yet clearly they would be considered part of the relevant public under, say, Rawls' theory of justice.[13]

To recap, a policy's public consists of two sets of persons: (1) those persons who are in a position to make the actual decision as to whether and when to bring about conditions C which occasion the agent's doing X; (2) those persons who are defined as part of the relevant public under the political and/or moral systems within which the agent makes the policy decision. Whether a particular policy is properly declared and revised so as not to violate the policy depends, then, on just what political and moral systems one perceives as the context within which the policy is located. Further, it should be noted that these two subsets of the relevant public may or may not intersect. Within a "pure" democracy, the first subset would be entailed by the second, and the second set would include all the people; within a capricious totalitarian system, the first and second sets would rarely intersect, and the second set would likely be very small indeed, i.e., only the views of the capricious power holders would, at least in their perceptions, likely be "due" consideration.

[13] To say that a political or moral system does not count all persons as members of the relevant public is *not*, of course, to say that membership in the relevant public *ought* to be thus restricted.

On the basis of this analysis of the term 'relevant public,' we may refine the fourth policy condition to read as follows:

> *The authorizing agent's obligation can be revised and yet not be violated* both *if the authorizing agent announces his revision of the conditional imperative from* I *to* I′ *to those persons who can bring about conditions* C *and* C′ and *if the authorizing agent gives consideration due the views of the relevant public as defined by the political and moral contexts of the initial policy decision and its revision.*

SUMMARY

At the outset we noted that this book treats policy as action rather than as behavior. That is, while policies can be described as "process outputs" or "patterns of response" or in other such behavioral terms, an interest in policy as something one undertakes with particular intention and purposes in mind renders a description of policy as a category of action, such as a plan, more appropriate. This choice of action language in no way is meant to deprecate the use of behavior language in other contexts. Much as an action description can suggest needed behavior-description research, research under a behavior description can be used to inform the policy-maker's action. The choice of action language here is based only on appropriateness in the context of a concern with policies as they are part and parcel of human action, i.e., of things people try to do.

In an attempt to distinguish 'policy' from related concepts such as plan, program, goal, principle of action, and promise, we generated four policy conditions. Then, so that the analysis might be made rigorous enough to help us to distinguish educational policies from policies in general (chapter 2) and to identify the fundamental issues of policy making (chapters 3 through 5), we refined the four policy conditions by extending the analysis of selected elements of the respective conditions. As developed and refined those four policy conditions are as follows:

> **Condition 1.** *Some authorizing agent (A$_a$) obligates itself to direct some implementing agent (A$_i$) to act in accord with a specified conditional imperative (I).*
>
> **Condition 2.** *The conditional imperative (I) must be of the form, Do something which counts as some specified X-ing whenever, without exception, specified conditions C occur.*
>
> **Condition 3.** *The authorizing agent (A$_a$) undertakes the obligation (condition 1) for the purpose of effecting some specified state of affairs (S) and to do so without violating any restrictive rules (R) by which A$_a$ would claim to abide.*
>
> **Condition 4.** *The authorizing agent's obligation can be revised and yet not be violated* both *if the authorizing agent announces his revision of the conditional imperative from I to I' to those persons who can bring about conditions C and C' and if the authorizing agent gives consideration due the views of the relevant public as defined by the political and moral contexts of the initial policy decision and its revision.*

This is to say, if some plan or program meets the first three conditions, then it counts as a policy, providing that it is revisable without violation in the manner specified in the fourth condition.

TWO
THE NATURE
OF
EDUCATIONAL POLICY

THE PROBLEM OF DISTINGUISHING EDUCATIONAL POLICY

OFTEN, PERHAPS TOO OFTEN, in our rush to say that we understand something, we resort to deflecting difficult questions in one or both of two ways. The first deflective device consists in our glossing over the surface when we have a hunch that a problem lies just below the surface. One use of such a deflective device might be to say that educational policies are distinguishable from other sorts of policies—welfare policies, taxing policies, medical policies, and so on —by the fact that educational policies are part and parcel of *educational* institutions. The suggestion here is that policies can correctly and instructively be classified according to the type of institution of which they are a part. According to this reasoning, welfare policies are designed and implemented by welfare departments; taxing policies are detailed by governmental tax-collection bureaus; and medical policies specify institutional actions taken within various sorts of medical institutions. With this "leger-de-mot" we almost make the problem of distinguishing educational policies from other policies disappear. There is indeed a ring of self-evidency in "policies of educational institutions are educational policies." But when we scratch the surface, it becomes clear that our gloss deflects a deepening of our understanding.

A well-placed question or two shows us that not all policies of educational institutions are *educational* policies; also, some educational policies do not fall under the aegis of educational institutions. To demonstrate these points, let us take a case of an educational institution, e.g., some university. While we could point to policies of that educational institution whch clearly seem to count as educational policies, such as the two-year "liberal education" policy, we can point to other university policies that we usually would not think of as educational policies, e.g., grounds-maintenance policies, support-staff personnel policies, and graduation-exercise policies. One is tempted to say that educational policies must, then, constitute but a subset of policies of educational institutions. But that does not solve the problem either, for some educational policies seem to fall outside the domain of those institutions that we commonly label "educational." Consider, for illustration, policies of the Federal Communications Commission. Though the FCC would not appear on the list of educational institutions, we would want, I think, to say that at least some of the FCC's policies which regulate commercial television's programming are clearly educational policies. If we are to take our concern with educational policies seriously, we must not allow the arbitrary limiting of educational policies to policies of educational institutions. To do so would be to leave ourselves open to having to study policies that are not of educational interest; further, we would be vulnerable to a form of myopia that eliminates from our fields of vision many potent educational policies.

The second deflective device would consist in our stipulating a definition of educational policy. Indeed, once it seems that a policy's being somehow attached to an educational institution is neither sufficient nor even necessary to the notion of educational policy, we are tempted to shelve the matter by saying, "By 'educational policy,' let us understand. . . ." The move seems attractive in that it rids us of our problem. Note, though, that when we make a stipulation, our propensity most often is perhaps to limit our attention to those policies of educational institutions which define the educational programs therein. Now of course at least in one sense, should such a move be criticized, it can correctly be countered with Humpty Dumpty's comment: "When *I* use a word, it means just what I choose it to mean —neither more nor less." That is, to stipulate a definition is to state a rule for a game, where it is the stipulator's prerogative to make up the game. A "no, you can't" would correctly be countered by a "don't be silly; of course I can." What can be successfully criticized—a point that seems to me to be frequently overlooked—is the often misleading nature of such a stipulation. If, for example, a book purports to address American educational policy and then the discussion is limited to educational policies within educational institutions, has not the author unnecessarily risked limiting our view of that topic? In other words, we risk missing much of the point of a discussion of educational policies in general, i.e., an identification of the field over which our concern with educational policies *should* range.

So we see that the assumption that educational policies are educational-institution policies invites a misunderstanding of what constitutes an educational policy. And the same may be said of stipulated definitions. But are we in any better shape in suggesting that the pertinent question is, "How *should* we define educational policy?" Does not that question force the response, "That depends on how one chooses to define education." For example, if one regards education as a tool for bringing each person to develop a sense of duty to fulfill his respective function of state and to acquire the skills or knowledge that the particular function requires (such as is Plato's view of education in the *Republic*), then educational policies will appropriately consist of those arrangements that the governing group provides to serve as that sort of tool. If, on the other hand, one's point of reference is not the state but the individual, and if education is viewed as a tutorial arrangement for developing the pupil's sense of social duty, understanding of others, and tolerance for "natural" conditions, then educational policies should be considered a subclass of tutorial policies, as Rousseau would have it in *Emile*. Or if one thinks of education as being identical with the mode of training in Skinner's *Walden II,* through which individuals develop self-control and "socially viable" interests, attitudes, desires, and feelings, then educational policies are nothing more and nothing less than those policies which implement that mode of training for those outcomes. In these three views of education, we see three different answers as to what *should* be taken as the universe of educational policies.

Does this mean that if we wish to decide what should be understood to count as an educational policy, we must decide upon a view of education; and further, that until we agree upon a view of education, we cannot say what is to count as an educational policy? If the answer is yes, then it makes no sense to try to discuss educational policy in general, for what counts as educational policy depends upon one's particular theoretical description of education. If we are productively to continue this discussion without tying it to a single view of education, we shall have to be able to answer negatively.

There are, I think, two sorts of negative responses that one can make, only the second of which is defensible. The first goes as follows. The one feature that cuts across educational policies is their common purpose, i.e., to create conditions that are conducive to learning. At first glance, this way of giving a negative response seems promising, for a concern for bringing about learning does seem common to the various views of education. But the rub is that not just any learning counts as education under the respective views. So then, the "learning" way out of our difficulty does not have enough discriminating power to narrow our focus onto strictly educational policies. And at the same time, it narrows our focus too much, because policies that delimit *what* learning should be brought about (as well as the above-mentioned policies the purpose of which is to create conditions that are conducive to learning) would also seem to count as educational policies. So saying that all education is somehow learning does not extricate us from our predicament.

Much as one can talk of moral dilemmas without committing the discussion to any particular moral theory, one can talk of educational policies without placing the discussion in the context of any particular educational theory. That is, there can be found an objective contextual use, as well as a subjective contextual use of the term education and thus educational policy.[1] Or, still otherwise put, one can note that any particular educational policy must be bound to the context of some view of education without recommending any particular view. In order to develop this meta-view of

[1] For a clear, concise presentation of the distinction between objective and subjective uses of a term, see Jonas F. Soltis, *An Introduction to the Analysis of Educational Concepts* (Reading, Mass.: Addison-Wesley, 1968), p. 9.

educational policy, we shall have to identify the categories of "decisions" that must be made (consciously or not) no matter what one's view of education, if any education whatsoever is to be undertaken. For example, instead of asking what educational policies in the *Republic, Emile,* and *Walden II* have in common, we shall ask, if one wants to undertake systematically to educate under any description, what categories of policies would one have to make? Note that a response to this question cannot suggest that the logic or grammar of educational policies is any different from that of noneducational policies. That is, whatever else an educational policy is, it is clearly at least a policy. We shall not, then, be seeking a way to view educational policies as somehow logically or conceptually different from any other sorts of policies. Rather, we shall be concerned to identify the categories of policy that are logically necessary to the conduct of education under any view.

POLICIES NECESSARY TO THE CONDUCT OF EDUCATION

Almost anyone under a wide range of conditions can build something. One does not have to be an accomplished carpenter or stone mason to figure out a way to construct something out of whatever is available. That is, in some fashion anyone can build things, and can do so with no more than whimsical, on-the-spot decisions. On seeing an uncrumpled, worked over manuscript page atop the wastebasket, I might pick it up and make a paper airplane, throw it back into the wastebasket, and return to my work. But should one decide to undertake building things systematically, the whimsical and unplanned must yield to the deliberate and planned. Similarly, almost anyone under a wide range of conditions can do some educating. One does not have to be an accomplished educational theorist or guru to figure out a way to do some educating under whatever the conditions. And education might be left to whimsical, spontaneous decisions. But, as with building, should one choose to conduct education *systematically over time,* then one must deliberately plan ways for making the resolution of perennial decisions systematic. This is not to say, of course, that all decisions one must make when systematically educating or even when systematically building can be anticipated and decided in advance. If we are to make our enterprise systematic, however, then we shall have to decide upon devices for making systematic at least those categories of decisions that our enterprise presupposes. Chapter 1 addressed the nature of those devices, i.e., *policies.* The point of this section is to identify those categories of decisions that must somehow be made if we are to educate at all. Again, the connection between policies and those decisions that are necessary to the conduct of education is this: if education is to be conducted systematically, then one needs to devise policies that guide or indicate how to make those essential educational decisions.

In order to identify those categories of decisions that are necessary to the conduct of education under any substantive description whatsoever, we shall first have to construct a description of education that is general enough to be amenable to any particular view of education. Whether one views education as a form of initiation into a culture or particular public forms of experience,[2] as a mechanism for giving persons marketable skills,[3] as a way to enable persons

[2] For such views of education, see R. S. Peters' essay, "Education as Initiation," which appears, among other places, in his *Authority, Responsibility and Education* (London: George Allen & Unwin, 1973); and P. H. Hirst and R. S. Peters, *The Logic of Education* (London: Routledge & Kegan Paul, 1970).

[3] Reference here is to the position taken by proponents of career or vocational education. For a historical review and critical discussion, see Arthur G. Wirth's "Philosophical Issues in the Vocational Liberal Studies Controversy (1900–1917): John Dewey vs.

to "come to know themselves," [4] or in any of a very large number of other both defensible and not so defensible ways, it consists, *minimally*, in the development of some beliefs, attitudes, skills, dispositions, values, understandings, or tastes, or any combination of these. A critic might note that historically there are those who in the true Platonic tradition would say that the point of the highest form of education is none of these, but one's coming to know the Truth. The force of this tack derives from the claim that not just any belief, but True belief, is what is called for. So then our general description is still satisfactory, for with it we are claiming only what minimally must be the case for an enterprise to count as education. That is, in order to be engaged in education one must be trying to develop *at least* some belief, attitude, skill, disposition, value, understanding, or taste. Correlatively, if one is not trying to develop at least one of these, then one is not educating under any view.

With this general definition of education, we can identify the first category of decision that any education whatsoever presupposes. It should be recalled that in doing so we identify the first category of policy that any *systematic* education whatsoever presupposes. That is, if an attempt to develop at least some belief, attitude, etc., is logically necessary to education, then in order to educate one must at some logically prior point *select* for the enterprise a specific belief, attitude, etc., or some combination thereof. Much as a carpenter must decide what it is that he sets out to build, so one must decide what of these educational contents he wishes to try to develop if he is to engage in the conduct of education. This is *not*, of course, to suggest that one must

---

the Social Efficiency Philosophers," and Robert Sherman's "Vocational Education and Democracy," both in *Studies in Philosophy and Education* 8, no. 3 (Winter 1974): 169–82 and 205–23, respectively.

[4] This view ranges from the classical "know thyself" to the crass view of education as a sort of self-diagnosis according to which "the proper study of humankind is me."

choose the content carefully, justifiably, or even deliberately in order to educate. The point is only that one must somehow decide. If one wishes to conduct education systematically, though, he would have at least to make the choice deliberately, but not necessarily carefully or justifiably. That is, a policy that guides the selection of content or curriculum (henceforth, *curricular policy*) is necessary to systematic education and, as such, counts as one category of educational policy.

For example, the conditional imperative may logically be of the form, to educate second-graders in P.S. 92, work to develop the following: language skills as described by . . . , disposition to keep desks neat, respect for . . . , and so on. Or, for university-level courses a professor might have a policy, "whenever teaching Philosophy 101, try to develop basic skills of conceptual and discourse analysis," or some such. Even a national education commission might make an educational content policy, e.g., by tying federal grants to educational institutions to specified content or curriculum, which in effect decides content for the educator, unless of course the educator decides not to "go along" with the policy. Regardless of the level and justification of a content or curriculum policy, content policies constitute one category of policy that is necessary to the systematic conduct of education.

The second category of policy that is essential to education consists of those policies that guide or regulate the *manner* in which one attempts to develop the selected content.[5] Once one has decided to build a tree house, if one is actually to build it, he must go about it in *some* way. Likewise, once one has decided to develop particular educational contents, if one is actually to educate, he must go about it

[5] This category of educational policies should not be confused with the restrictive purposes (*R*-purposes) discussed in chapter 1.

in some way. The range of possible manners is wide. Just what manner one would select would seem to depend upon three things: (1) one's beliefs about the epistemological ordering of the selected content; (2) one's beliefs about the psychological ordering of the pupil's mind; and (3) one's repertoire of pedagogic methods. One might, for example, believe that "mathematical propositions are *constitutive* of scientific propositions insofar as mathematics constitutes part of the 'grammar' through which scientific propositions are structured and expressed." [6] Were this so, then in order to develop particular scientific beliefs, one might choose to go about that educative talk via the route of mathematics. Further, if one believed that the child in whom particular beliefs are to be nurtured has the requisite cognitive structures [7] to comprehend one type of explanation and not another, then one would select to try to develop the beliefs through one rather than another sort of explanation. And, if for some reason one prized a particular pedagogic method (ranging widely from classical conditioning to rational inquiry) more than others, then he would reasonably select that method rather than any other.

To be sure, some thoughtful educators would never resort to techniques of classical conditioning, much less even allow them to count as educative methods. And some would choose to limit the manner of education to rational, critical

[6] This example is Richard Pring's in his "Curriculum Integration," in *The Philosophy of Education*, ed. R. S. Peters (Oxford: Oxford University Press, 1973), p. 147.

[7] Today, talk of the psychological ordering of the content of education brings to mind the works of Piaget and Kohlberg in particular. An earlier (1902) discussion of the distinction between the logical order of subject matter (epistemological order) and the psychological order of subject matter and its importance in the deciding of pedagogic methodology is to be found in John Dewey's *The Child and the Curriculum* (Chicago: University of Chicago Press, Phoenix Edition, 1956), esp. pp. 19–31.

inquiry.[8] But the moral reasons for selecting one rather than another pedagogic method of educating are beside the point here. And clearly there are reasons in addition to moral ones for selecting one method over another. One method, for example, may be more effective or efficient than another for learners with different characteristics.[9] Indeed, the considerations that can go into deciding how the particular educational content is to be developed are numerous and complex. The point of noting these is to demonstrate that if we are to educate systematically, we must not only decide upon content or curricular policies, but also on policies that regulate the manner of how we go about trying to develop beliefs, attitudes, etc. With the reminder that concerns with manner include epistemological and psychological issues as well as pedagogic methods, let us call this second category of policies that are necessary to the conduct of education *methodological policies.*

Frequently, when talk of education focuses on teaching only, curricular and methodological policies are mistaken as the only policies that are necessary to systematic education. What seems to be so commonly missed when education is reduced to teaching are the institutional arrangements that provide the immediate context for the conduct of education. Now it may not seem obvious that institutional arrangements are necessary for the conduct of education. To be sure, if one is concerned only with occasional, whimsical, or as-the-opportunity-presents-itself edu-

[8] For a number of excellent philosophical essays which are permeated with this view and which are now conveniently collected into a single volume, see Israel Scheffler, *Reason and Teaching* (Indianapolis: Bobbs-Merrill, 1973).

[9] For a review of work on this topic (sometimes labeled "aptitude-treatment interaction"), see L. J. Cronbach and R. E. Snow, "Individual Differences in Learning Ability as a Function of Instructional Variables" (Final Report, School of Education, Stanford University, Contract No. OEC–4–6–061269–1217, U.S. Office of Education, 1969. ERIC ED 029001).

cation, then institutional arrangements are not necessary. But if one desires to conduct education systematically over time, then it is essential to have some regular allocation or dedication of some sorts of learning resources.[10] It is, I believe, an empirical fact that in order to assure the allocation or dedication of resources to the conduct of education, one must make particular institutional arrangements. That is, one must embed the enterprise in the context of institutions, those more enduring social structures. The means for doing that is the making of institutional policies that assign particular resources to education. In other words, institutional arrangements are not logically necessary to the systematic conduct of education because they are institutional; what is necessary is the regular allocation of resources. While keeping in mind that the vehicle for establishing the regular allocation of resources is commonly the institution, we shall call the third category of educational policies *resource-allocation policies* or simply *resource policies*.

It might further be noted that the nature of the educational-resource institution, the educative potency of that institution relative to the other social institutions, and the nature of resources dedicated to the institution all affect how well or poorly education is conducted. If, for example, the conduct of education is limited to school undertakings and if the educational potency of schools is weak relative to other social institutions, such as commercial television, and if few and often inappropriate resources are allocated to the schools, then we could not reasonably expect education to be conducted as well as it might be if the institutional arrangements were otherwise. Resource-allocation policies are not, then, to be taken as merely intrainstitutional regulations,

[10] I borrow the felicitous term 'learning resources' from Kenneth Silber et al., "The Field of Educational Technology: A Statement of Definition," *Audiovisual Instruction* 17, no. 8 (October 1972): 38–39.

but also as interinstitutional rules that define the relative resource priority of the institution or combination of institutions which undertake the conduct of education.

The fourth category of policies that seem necessary to
the systematic conduct of education responds to the question,
whose beliefs, attitudes, skills, dispositions, values, understandings, or tastes are to be developed? The question asks
who is to receive the educational benefits of our conduct of
education. Or, more simply, just who is to be educated?
Much as it seems obvious that one must select some content
if one is to educate, so it seems perspicuous that one must
select some "whom" to be educated. One of the logical conditions of 'giving,' 'presenting,' 'offering,' and 'educating'
is a someone to whom the action is directed. A *selection* is
necessary by the following reasoning: (1) some person to
whom the action is directed is logically necessary to the concept of education, (2) there are literally billions of persons
to whom such action could be directed, and (3) in practice
(if only because of scarcity of resources and the relatively
puny nature of present institutions dedicated to education)
the conduct of education can hardly be directed toward the
development of beliefs, attitudes, etc., of *all* persons; one
must select potential benefactors for any educative effort.
Clearly this is so.

But one might question whether a policy that governs
the distribution of educational benefits counts *only* as an
educational policy. Might it not serve as well as a social
stratification policy or as a political policy of another sort? I
grant the point, but I would add that simply because a policy
can be described as more than one sort of policy does not
reduce the validity of use of any one of the descriptions.
That is, the fact that policies that regulate the distribution of
educational benefits (henceforth, *distributional policies*)
might be seen not only as educational policies, but also as

political policies does not alter their status as policies that are essential to the conduct of education. It is important to be clear about this point, especially if one wants to claim that, say, citizens have a right to particular sorts of educational benefits. Such a claim cannot be dismissed by noting that distributional policies are *really* just political issues. They are no more *really* "just political" than they are educational. If in deciding on a policy for the distribution of educational benefits, one must make some sort of a "political" decision, then such is sometimes the nature of educational policy decisions.

To recap, the policies that are necessary to the systematic conduct of education are content or *curricular policies, methodological policies, resource policies*, and *distributional policies.* Any one of these policies may or may not be made within the schools, academies, colleges, and universities, i.e., those structures we call our educational institutions. For example, in deciding that the New Soviet Man was to have particular beliefs, attitudes, understandings, values, tastes, etc., and that the goal of Soviet education was to be the creation of New Soviet Men, the Communist Party shaped the basic curricular policies of education in the Soviet Union. Here the educational policy derives, not from an educational institution, but from a political party. For a second example, consider the Supreme Court's decision in *Brown* v. *Board of Education of Topeka, Kansas,* in which a resource policy was made: *equal protection* was reinterpreted from "separate but equal" to "the same facilities for all." Again, the policy clearly counts as an educational policy under our analysis, but would not so count if we were arbitrarily to limit educational policies to the so-called educational institutions. For however tedious this development of categories has been, it will perhaps keep us from narrowing our focus to schooling alone. To do so clearly would make us blind to numerous very important educational problems and policies.

THE NESTING OF EDUCATIONAL POLICIES

Anyone who has ever tried to locate and evaluate educational policies might find our identification of the four categories of educational policies helpful, especially in locating those educational policies that fall outside the walls of educational institutions. But anyone who has ever tried to study educational policies would likely be quick to note that the four categories are of little help when trying to survey policy options. That is, the recognition of the need for some curricular policy, for example, does not tell us anything about the range of admissible policy choices. Any elementary school teacher who is worth his salt can tell you that when he is considering a revision of his curricular policy for the ensuing academic year, the range of curricular policies that are admissible is not without limit. The district curricular policy might require that particular skills be taught, and the state board of instruction may have a policy that requires teachers to limit the bulk of their teaching time to a specified set of subject matters. Whether of the curricular, methodological, resource, or distributional category, this policy seems to be somehow "nested" in other policies. The phenomenon is not, as may first be thought, limited to policies made within public institutions of education. State and federal laws (governmental and political system policies) even limit the allowable range of curricular content of parents' educative policies for their children. For example, one federal law (the Smith Act) prohibits, among other things, parents' teaching beliefs and attitudes that incite their children to attempt to overthrow violently the federal government. I grant that there are few such laws; nonetheless, there are some and that fact supports my point: at least on the teaching level, educational policies are nested in other policies of the same category.

That the nesting of educational policies seems to be a common phenomenon provides one good reason for considering it more closely. And because when making any educational policy that is nested in another policy or policies, one must somehow take those other policies into account, it seems important even in the most practical sense that we examine the way in which policies are related when one is nested in another. Just to say that they are somehow related is true, but uninformative and uninstructive. The question is, what must be true to say that policy A is nested in policy B?

To begin, let us return to the example of the second-grade teacher who is considering revisions of his curricular policy for the next academic year. He is mulling over the question of what skills, beliefs, understandings, etc., he wants to try to help the new students to develop. The full range of logically possible contents is far too large to tackle. He wishes to make a careful selection of content and to write those contents into a policy that will then guide him in his day-to-day teaching. On checking the state curricular policy for the second grade, he sees that the admissible contents do not in fact range over all logical possibilities, but are limited to those contents that can be somehow included in a course of instruction detailed in the *Elementary School Syllabi: Grade-level Curricula*. Unless the teacher decides to act contrary to the state curricular policy and risk dismissal, he will consider his actual range of choice for his curricular policy (policy A) limited to the range specified in the state curricular policy (policy B). That is, policy A is nested in policy B when policy B limits the range of admissible policy A candidates.

Now, it does seem clear that sometimes the B-A policy relationship is a limiting one. But is it always? Consider the following hypothetical case. Thanks to a new district policy, a teacher who once had at his disposal for teaching purposes only a few textbooks, the town library, and a few phonograph records now has a computer terminal, audio- and video-tape recorders, slide projectors, and a substantial paperback library. His policy regarding the use of learning resources used to be limited to the very meager resources of his financially poorly endowed school and community. The new district policy, which makes the additional resources available at the teacher's request, could hardly be said to *limit* the teacher's choice of resource policy, yet we would want to say that the teacher's resource policy is nested in that of the district. In this case, policy B seems to *expand*, rather than limit, the range of choice for policy A. The nesting condition should, then, be rewritten to state: policy A is nested in policy B when B *limits or expands the range of admissible or factually possible policy* A *candidates*. A note of caution and qualification is in order. Care should be taken to avoid confusing a nesting relationship with a complete and exact prescription. That is, if policy B tells the teacher exactly, no more and no less, what resources he must use, then there exists but one resource policy, i.e., policy B, and so there can logically be no nesting relationship. The teacher might have a policy of acting in accord with policy B, but that does not constitute a separate resource policy. That is, policy A is nested in policy B when B limits or expands the range of admissible or factually possible policy A candidates, *excepting when* B *prescribes in exact detail what agent* A *is to do*.

Having identified the four categories of educational policies and having established the conditions under which one policy of any given category of policy is correctly said to be nested in another, we are ready to turn to an examination of the purposes, authorizing agents, and relevant publics

of educational policies: curricular, methodological, resource, and distributional.

THE PURPOSES OF EDUCATIONAL POLICIES

As noted, the underlying purpose of any policy is to
make systematic some enterprise. The same may be said of
educational policies in particular. If one had no interest in
the *systematic* conduct of education, then one should have
no concern with educational *policies*. Further, we noted,
there are four logically necessary categories of decisions that
one must somehow make if one is to educate in any fashion,
though in unsystematic education these decisions may be
made by default, or may actually be made but not deliberately or even consciously made. But one way or another,
when one educates one selects content to be developed,
method to be employed, resources to be used, and a distribution for the educational benefits. If we opt for the systematic conduct of education, then not just any way of
making these decisions will do. Specifically, in choosing to
conduct education systematically, one makes four categories
of *policy* decisions necessary to the enterprise: curricular
policies, methodological policies, resource policies, and distributional policies. To inquire into the nature of the purposes of educational policies is to request more than what is
the purpose of policies. It is to ask what descriptively might
be said about the purposes of the four respective categories
of educational policies. And since there are different sorts of
purposes that policies can have, part of that discussion of
the purposes of educational policies shall include identification of what type of purpose each category of educational
policy might be expected to have. Still further, it shall be
instructive to distinguish purposes by the location of the
policies in the "nesting."

As our analysis of educational policies does indeed throughout (*ana-*) loosen (*lyein*) the whole into its parts, we are faced with progressively more and more distinctions to keep in mind: categories of educational policies, types of policy purposes, and different orders in the nesting of policies. In order to keep track of these distinctions so that we might use them to clarify the purposes of educational policies, let us employ a graphic representation of the intersections of these distinctions (figure 1). The four categories of

Category of Educational Policy	Location in Nesting	Types of Purposes			
		S-purposes			R-purposes
		Unachievable	Once Achievable	Repeatedly Achievable	
Curricular	Outermost				
	Innermost				
Methodological	Outermost				
	Innermost				
Resource	Outermost				
	Innermost				
Distributional	Outermost				
	Innermost				

Figure 1

educational policy were developed earlier in this chapter (under "Policies Necessary to the Conduct of Education"), so no further comment is required here. But while we did discuss the nesting of policies, the "outermost" and "innermost" locations of policies in a nesting need further discussion. Then, without adding to the discussion of types of purposes of policies (see chapter 1, "What Can Count as a

Policy's Purpose?"), we will briefly review those types of purposes.

In considering what must be true to say that policy A is nested in policy B, we uncovered the conditions under which one policy counts as being more "inner" (perspective from policy A) or more "outer" (perspective from policy B) than another policy. In order to have the graphic representation of our distinctions cover the full range of possible nestings of educational policies, it is convenient to identify the logically innermost and outermost policies. If the overall purpose of education is taken as being the development of skills, attitudes, understandings, and so forth, then it would seem that no policies can be more "inner" than those which guide that enterprise the point of which is to take the final steps toward developing those skills, attitudes, understandings, etc. That is, there appears to be no educationally more inner activity than teaching. The innermost educational policies would, then, consist of the curricular, methodological, resource, and distributional policies of teaching.

To locate the logically outermost enterprise the conduct of which might be regulated by educational policies, we must point to the most encompassing, highest level of governance of the social and political order. Just why this is so may not be obvious. The line of reasoning goes this way: If for policy A to be nested in policy B, policy B must limit or expand the allowable policy As, and not the other way around, then policy B supersedes policy A. If one policy (B) supersedes another (A), it does so by virtue of the fact that the authority of agent B is of a higher order than that of A. Just as policies that do not carry the force of law are superseded by those that do, and as policies that are laws of a lower governing unit are superseded by those of the higher unit, educational policies that do not carry the force of law are superseded by those that do and those that do carry the force of law are "most superseded" by the highest level of law. This line of reasoning brings us to the conclusion that the outermost educational policy in a nesting would be that of the highest governmental level. In the present political order of the world, the outermost educational policies would be those of federal or national governments.

Two caveats should be borne in mind. First, while educational policies of teaching are logically the innermost and educational policies of the federal government are logically the outermost, this is not to say that in every instance a teaching-level educational policy or a federal educational policy actually exists. Such would be so only if education were conducted in the most systematic way possible. Second, the fact that a teaching-level policy or a federal educational policy (or both) of a particular category does not actually exist in a given instance does not warrant the inference that on no level does an educational policy of that category exist. For example, just because a teacher has developed no policy to govern his selection of educational resources and because the federal government has created no policy to govern the allocation of educational resources, our inferring that no resource policy exists is not warranted. A school principal, a school board, or a state office of education might have such a policy. That is, the point of focusing on the logically innermost and outermost educational policies is *not* to claim that such policies always do or should exist. Rather, to focus on the logical extremes should be construed only as a move toward convenience in analysis.

The reader will recall from chapter 1 that unachievable policy purposes consist of perfect states of affairs which are not to be achieved—their achievement is logically impossible—but to be imitated more and more exactly as is possible. A policy that has a once-achievable purpose can no longer have that purpose once it has been achieved, while a policy with a repeatedly achievable purpose is fulfilling its purpose only if by means of that policy some state of affairs

is being effected again and again. In that these purposes
are describable only with reference to some state of affairs,
we called them S-purposes which are to be contrasted with
R-purposes, i.e., those restrictive purposes which an authorizing agent may impose to regulate the manner in which
the S-purpose may be achieved. It should be remembered
that while an S-purpose logically can stand alone as a policy's purpose, an R-purpose cannot.

Let us first attend to the purposes of the outermost educational policies, i.e., those purposes of logically possible (if
not always actual) federal educational policies. The purpose of an outermost curricular policy might be, for example, to develop those contents (skills, understandings, etc.)
that would bring about a state of affairs in which persons are
able to exercise fully their First Amendment rights. Here
"exercise *fully*" suggests that the purpose is unachievable.
That is, no matter to what degree one is able to exercise his
First Amendment rights, he could always become more able
to exercise those rights still more fully by acquiring yet
higher levels of verbal skills, by developing a clearer understanding of how to redress grievances, or by acquiring still
more sophisticated publication skills and the like. In that
the elements of ability to exercise First Amendment rights
admit of ever higher degrees and in that the purpose is
stated as an ideal, the purpose is approachable but unachievable. Indeed, unachievability of S-purposes appears
to be a typical feature of candidates for federal curricular
policies. This commonly unachievable nature of outermost
policies has frequently been mistaken for and conflated with
intangibility, lack of clarity, and vagueness.[11] If by tangible
is to be understood "measurable," then surely those educa-

---

[11] For a discussion of the sort with which I take issue here,
see Rachel Elboim Dror's treatment of educational goals in "Some
Characteristics of the Educational Policy Formation System," *Policy
Sciences* 1, no. 2 (Summer 1970): esp. 232–37.

tional contents that enable one to exercise First Amendment rights are tangible. There need be no muddle, I think, about what constitutes a First Amendment right and about what educational contents would contribute to an exercise thereof. The claim of vagueness derives, I submit, from a confounding of vagueness with generality. The First Amendment is, thank goodness, general, as might be any statement of educational contents that would enable one to exercise those rights. Generality does not logically entail vagueness.

The purpose of outermost methodological policy would likely be limited to the effecting of a state of affairs in which educational methodology reflects the methodology of the political system. For example, in a purportedly democratic political system, one would expect the outermost methodological policy to aspire toward some purely democratic method of developing the selected content. And, once again, by the same reasoning as before, the purpose would appear to be of an unachievable nature. Historically, though, there have been cases in which the ideology of the political system has prescribed in some detail what psychological claims and, hence, pedagogical methodology are "correct," as in the Lysenko period in the Soviet Union. During that period, the politically highest body limited the range of allowable methodological policies by politically prescribing particular empirical claims rather than leaving their fate to the test of empirical inquiry. That is, the purpose of the outermost methodological policy was a doctrinal ideal.

While one would expect the purposes of the outermost curricular and methodological policies to be unachievable, the same does not hold for the purposes of resource and distributional policies. Let us consider them in turn. The potentially most powerful yet most undeveloped category of educational policy (at least in the United States) would appear to be outermost resource policies. On the federal or national level, the allocation of resources of any kind is most radically alterable, whether the issue be energy resources, defense resources, educational resources, or any of a large number of other sorts of resources. To focus on educational resources, one needs to consider those communications networks and institutions which by their nature have marked educative potency and over which the federal government has or might exercise control. An example of one such educationally potent resource is television programming, over which the federal government has some formal control through the Federal Communications Commission.

Not only is the federal government in a position to take a remarkably large role in the allocation of educational resources, it is also in a position to increase radically the pool of educational resources, depending upon where educational resources are placed in the listing of federal budgetary priorities. In those countries in which the federal or national government systematically engages in the conduct of education, the purposes appear to be repeatedly achievable and, generally, of the form, "whenever dedicating federally controlled resources to governmental enterprises, grant education X percent." Or, possibly, "whenever a resource has exceptional educative potency, place that resource under federal regulation." In these cases, the purpose is to achieve a state of affairs, planning period after planning period, in which a particular portion of federal resources is dedicated to the systematic conduct of education and to commit particular types of educationally potent resources to the systematic conduct of education. My intent here is not to prescribe the establishment of educational resource policies on the federal level, but to point out what would likely be the nature of the purposes of such logically possible educational policies.

The fourth category of outermost educational policies consists of distributional policies, i.e., those policies that regulate who are to receive the educational benefits (or "malefits," depending on one's view) of the systematic conduct of education. The purpose of an outermost distributional policy would likely be to bring about a state of affairs in which the social stratification fits a particular description, or in which the distribution of "needed" skills satisfies some national criterion, or in which the educational benefits are evenly distributed over all sex, race, age, or other groupings. Such purposes appear to be perennially achievable, if they are achievable at all. My hunch, supported by the Coleman report and the Jencks study, is that if such purposes as the latter are ever to be achievable in practice, a very strong and generous federal resource-allocation policy would have to be established. Logically, of course, distributional policies such as these are achievable and repeatedly so.

I suspect that at this point a reflective pause is in order. One might wonder at the sense of surveying "outermost" or federal educational policies that do not exist. What on earth has such a survey to do with the analysis of educational policies? The question needs response, for if the point of an analysis of educational policy is not to help us make sense of, to criticize, and to develop *actual* educational policy, then what is the point? My response is this. By considering at least the logical possibility of federal educational policy and what conceivably might constitute such policy, we place ourselves in a better position to respond to such questions as: Should there be a federal educational resource policy? Or, what should be the nature and scope of federal educational policies? The point of this essay is not to offer substantive response to such questions.[12] Rather, it is to provide a framework in which the sense of asking such questions

---

[12] For such a substantive discussion, see Harry L. Summerfield, *Power and Process: The Formulation and Limits of Federal Educational Policy* (Berkeley: McCutchan, 1974), esp. chap. 6.

might be made clearer (this chapter) and to suggest considerations that should enter into substantive responses to such questions (chapters 3 through 5).

Having surveyed the nature of purposes of the various outermost educational policies, let us now turn to the innermost policies, i.e., those policies which guide teaching in the systematic conduct of education. As might be suspected, more of a specific nature has appeared in the literature of philosophy of education on teaching policies than on nonexistent federal policies in the conduct of education. Those discussions, though, fall short of covering the four categories of teaching policies that are necessary to the systematic conduct of education. (This is, of course, not to say that they fall short of doing what they set out to do.)

Let us consider, for example, what must be true to say that someone (T) is teaching in Scheffler's analysis: [13] (1) T must intend to bring about some learning; (2) the method that T uses must be reasonably likely to bring about the intended learning; and (3) that method must be morally acceptable. In terms of the distinctions of our analysis, this is to say, in order to teach, one must select some content and make a methodological decision that is limited by a restrictive purpose of a particular nature. Green's view differs mainly in that he would dispense with the restrictive purpose (the moral acceptability of the method) to free the "teaching continuum" of an "a priori normative definition." [14] On the chart of distinctions (figure 1), teaching in these views would be represented as follows, with the difference consisting in Scheffler's requiring a methodological R-purpose of a specified sort, while Green would not. Further, for an

[13] Israel Scheffler, *The Language of Education* (Springfield, Ill.: Charles C Thomas, 1960), chap. 4.
[14] Thomas F. Green, "A Typology of the Teaching Concept," *Studies in Philosophy and Education* 3, no. 4 (Winter 1964): 293.

Category of Policy and Location in Nesting	S-purposes			R-purposes
	Unachiev- able	Once Achievable	Repeatedly Achievable	
Curricular, innermost		X		
Methodological, innermost		X		[X]

Figure 2

activity to count as teaching in this minimal sense, only curricular and methodological *decisions* but not *policy decisions* are necessary. Further, a once-achievable purpose would suffice for both the curricular and methodological decisions.

The point here of alluding to the Scheffler and Green analyses of 'teaching' is not to criticize those analyses. Rather, it is to enable us to ask, what in addition to teaching in this minimal sense would one have to do in order to be engaging systematically in the conduct of education? Or, more simply put, what in addition to teaching in the minimal sense would one have to do to be teaching in a maximal or most systematic sense? By looking at the necessary yet empty categories on the chart, we see that *additionally* two conditions would have to obtain: (1) the content and methodological decisions would have to be policy decisions; (2) T must be acting in accord with resource and distributional teaching policies as well. That is, for one to be teaching in the maximal sense, one must actually make a decision of each of the categories of decisions that are necessary to the conduct of education, *and* those decisions must be made systematically, i.e., according to a policy. Further, it might be noted that while one might have in mind once-achievable purposes, if he were to view his task *not* as one of bringing about acontextual, discrete, unrelated learnings by discrete and unrelated learners, and if he does view as his task the education of a number of persons over time, then the purpose of his undertakings would have to be repeatedly achievable.

Especially those who have had considerable teaching experience will recognize the very high level of sophistication that teaching in this strong sense would require. In this view it is not enough that the teacher try to bring about just *some* learning via *some* method that is likely to bring about that learning. The teacher must decide in a particular way (i.e., by acting in accord with a policy) what learning is to be brought about and (in accord with another policy) how that learning is to be brought about. Moreover, the teacher must select according to still another policy the resources to employ in that teaching as well as to what learners the teaching is to be directed.

In effect, this strong sense of teaching requires that the teaching be conducted on the basis of policy and not arbitrary decisions, mere hunches, and trial and error. Further, it moves pedagogic experimentation from usual teaching decisions to those decisions that go into deciding what the policies are to be. If the "state of the art" is not presently such that teaching can contribute to the systematic conduct of education, then I suspect that for the time we must be satisfied with only that degree of systematicness that our teaching sophistication is up to. Though I will not argue in support of the claim, it is, I think, clearly desirable for educational decisions, whether innermost or outermost, to be conducted in a manner in which the decision component of each action is justifiable by appeal to some policy which is, in turn, both rational and just. So, as in our consideration of the outermost policies in the nesting, we are here faced with the curious circumstance of trying to describe policies that in large measure do not exist. But, as noted, it makes good sense to survey the purposes of these logically possible if not always actual, educational policies. Chapters 3 through 5 discuss what considerations in particular would be constitutive of the deliberations for determining what policies are rational and just.

Our present question is this: what is the nature of the purposes of curricular, methodological, resource, and distributional policies that are embedded in teaching as part of the systematic conduct of education? Recall that one of the four policy conditions states that the agent undertakes the obligation for the purpose of effecting some specified state of affairs (S) and to do so without violating any restrictive rules (R) by which the agent would claim to abide. Given that the logically innermost educational policies are teaching policies, any policies that are more "outer" in the nesting with which the teacher as agent of the innermost policy would claim to comply may define at least some of the restrictive purposes of the teaching policies. Such would be the case whenever the more outer policy limits rather than expands the range of allowable or practically possible, respectively, teaching policies.

Thus, in order to determine the R-purposes of any inner policy, one would have to examine the ways in which the more outer policies are limiting. For example, should a more outer curricular policy limit an innermost curricular policy by not allowing a discussion of specified "controversial issues," and if the agent of the latter policy claims to abide by the limitations of the former, then whatever state(s)-of-affairs purpose the teacher might have in mind, he will also have the R-purpose of restricting teaching so as not to include those controversial issues. Clearly, the teacher's curricular policy might have other R-purposes, such as satisfying a criterion of moral acceptability. The main point here is that as an educational activity, teaching may be nested in the context of other policies. By virtue of that fact, whenever the more outer policies limit the allowable range of the more inner policy, the R-purposes of the more inner policy are determined at least in part by the more outer policy. The same point could be exemplified with methodological, resource, and distributional policies as well.

Thus we see that the restrictive purposes of the more inner policies can derive from the S-purposes of the more outer policies. Might a similar generalization be made about the S-purposes of the more inner policies? We shall see that the answer is negative. That is, while the more outer policies can restrict or expand the range of admissible inner-policy candidates, they logically cannot specify the S-purpose of the more inner policy. Initially the claim may seem odd. Surely the school board, for example, can require a teacher to adopt a particular school policy. Is not that in fact what happens when a school board has a curricular policy that prescribes detailed grade-level content syllabi? In this instance, the innermost curricular policy was made, not on the teaching level, but on the district level; and the teacher has become an implementing agent in the district's curricular policy for teaching. The point may not be obvious, but it is important to bear in mind when trying to sort out educational policies. For a person to adopt any policy, there must be a range of more than one allowable course of action. If a particular curriculum and methodology has been made "teacher proof," to use a term of some currency, then the teacher logically can have no curricular or methodological policy. The only decision that remains concerns whether to play the teaching game at all, given those rules.

Having clarified the relationship of the inner policy purposes to the outer ones, we are now ready to survey the purposes of the innermost policies that are necessary to the systematic conduct of education. As before, let us begin with the curricular policies. One point of such policies would seem to be that of bringing about a state of affairs in which (1) there is a basis for deciding the educational content for cases of teaching and (2) the educational content of any instance of teaching would be justifiable by appeal to a curricular policy which, presumably, could thus be more care-fully decided than if the content decision were left to be dealt with solely on a case-by-case basis. Such S-purposes derive from the definition of curricular policies. There might be additional S-purposes, e.g., the teacher may have in mind the purpose of holding the content of his teaching to those contents which he feels most competent to treat. Further, any teacher likely values some allowable skills, under-standings, appreciations, etc., more than others and may wish to bring about a state of affairs in which others have acquired his favored educational contents. Other S-pur-poses of curricular policy may regard not content itself, but other matters that the teacher may deem important. For example, a teacher may have a policy of altering the content of his courses each year, not for curricular reasons, but for the purpose of maintaining a state of affairs in which the variety is such that he can keep his sanity and still continue to teach year after year. One suspects that it is the S-purposes of such curricular teaching policies which do not regard content that are overlooked when the innermost curricular decisions are removed from the teacher's control. Policies that standardize in detail the content to be taught typically disregard the individual teacher's content fortes and rele-vant psychological needs, e.g., the not uncommon need for some variety.

The primary S-purpose of the innermost methodological policies is, by definition, to provide a way for selecting a methodology for the development of the specified content. Primarily one would expect that choice to be based on criteria of efficiency and effectiveness, i.e., that primary pur-pose would be to bring about a state of affairs in which the methods employed are both efficient and effective. But as in the case of curricular policies, any teacher likely has other S-purposes for which he designs any methodological policies —purposes which, as before, may regard his own pedagogic skill-development and his desire to make the teaching enterprise one that he can live with over time. Some such purposes are clearly defensible as purposes in educational policies in that they are relevant to the health of the conduct of education and so clearly ought not to be disregarded, even though they may be personal in nature.

If one is aware of (1) how little solid empirical work presently exists to provide empirical grounds for choosing one method over another in the teaching of particular sorts of things to particular learners and (2) the lingering lack of an effective mechanism for getting what we collectively know about the relative merits of different methodologies into the heads of teachers, he may at this point be tempted to sigh at the seeming naïveté of the suggestion that teachers could ever know enough even to make a sound methodological choice from time to time, much less to make sound methodological policies which involve choices for classes of decision points. A "counter sigh" might be in order: We do not yet know enough to conduct education systematically in every detail, maybe not even in gross ways. But if we are ever to learn how, we shall have to learn enough to establish methodological policies, for to establish sound *policies* regarding methodology is to think through carefully how methodological decisions ought to be handled in order to take advantage of what we do know empirically when we are thinking most clearly, i.e., before we are caught in the pressures of the on-the-spot conduct of education. Further, it might be argued that if the conduct of education is worth our while, then it is worth our doing as intelligently as we know how. This is to say, it is at least worth guiding with carefully wrought policies.

If it is difficult to believe that in practice there is hope for the establishment of curricular and methodological teaching policies, then it shall be even more difficult to believe that it makes sense even to talk of resource policies for teaching. Resources are classroom "givens," are they not? One who teaches in "the real world of the public schools" [15] doubtless would find humorless the suggestion that there are sufficient educational resources in number and variety at their disposal for the establishment of policies regarding resources to make sense. By definition, the general point of a resource policy in teaching is to guide intelligently the selection of educational resources through which the selected content is to be developed with the chosen methodology. Such a policy seems to assume the existence of something that does not presently exist, namely, a nontrivial choice among possible resources.

One might spar with this imagined public school teacher by underscoring the fact that notable and varied educational resources *are* at the teacher's disposal. The problem rests, as the rejoinder goes, not in the lack of available educational resources. Often the textbooks are givens, but also available within the school system are the school library, a wide range of hardware (slide projectors to videotaping equipment) from, say, a district distribution center, and countless films which may be ordered through some regional public school office—not to mention the materials which fill the "supply closet" shelves. One could also enumerate non-school-system resources that are available for school use, e.g., the public libraries, public museums, and many private resources. The rejoinder would be that the problem rests, rather, in the teachers' lacking resource policies that would remind them of the nature and wide range of the educational resources which are available, though stored beyond the classroom walls.

Our public school teacher's reply at this point might

[15] For a nontechnical constructive criticism of that realm, see Harry S. Broudy, *The Real World of the Public Schools* (New York: Harcourt Brace Jovanovich, 1972).

consist of a concession that a wealth of resources is available "in theory," but also a reminder that those same resources are not available for practical purposes. That is, even if a teacher knew that an especially effective way to help a student develop delivery skills in public speaking, for example, is to video-tape the student's delivery and then to play back the tape for the student with critical commentary, the investment of time and energy required to obtain the needed equipment far outweighs the importance of that particular teaching task in light of other teaching tasks to which one must attend. The teacher's point, it seems to me, must be conceded. If resources are not available in a sense that would make their procurement for pedagogic use practicable, then we cannot count those resources as available for educational purposes. What this suggests is that wide-ranging resource policies for teaching will become actual possibilities only when more outer policies regarding resource allocation not only expand the range, but also increase the ease of availability of those resources. If the assumption that educational resources vary in their appropriateness to content and methodology is correct, then excellence in teaching will require a sufficient range of readily available resources and carefully designed teaching resource policies so that the resources might in fact be utilized with consistent appropriateness.

As we turn to a consideration of policies that are innermost in the nesting of distributional policies, our imagined public school teacher-critic may well be baffled. If one thing characterizes public schooling, it is its public nature. The schools must take all who come, providing they are of the proper age group. Further, some of those by force of law must come. And if one thing is common to all public school teaching, it is the fact that the teacher must accept into his classroom all those who are assigned and who, willingly or not, present themselves. While our critic might agree that the quality, intensity, and duration of the conduct of education may vary greatly between states, districts, schools, and even classrooms, he would hasten to point out that once the classroom door is closed, the teacher has no choice in the matter of who should receive the educational benefits of his teaching.

The critic's claim here, as in the case of resource policies, is that while it does make sense to concern ourselves with the distribution of education on "higher" levels, it does not on the teaching level. Ensuring a quality, intensity, and duration of the conduct of education in an inner-city school that matches that of a suburban school, attending to the development and maintenance of a specified racial integration of schools, seeing to the development of physical education for females that at least matches that for males, and the like, are all kinds of purposes to be served by distributional policies. But such policies clearly outstrip the authority of the individual classroom teacher. In short, our critic would argue, to search for the purposes of distributional policies in teaching is to try to find the present king of France.

Our critic is claiming, I think, more than is supportable. What his argument supports is the weaker claim that the distributional policies of individual teachers cannot alter the basic overall distribution which is set by the more outer distributional policies. To that point I see no counter. We would have to agree that the teacher clearly seems to be in no position to alter the composition of the class he faces, nor is he in a position to reassign the students to a more or less competent teacher. This is *not*, though, to agree that it is not within the teacher's province to affect the distribution of educational benefits in any way, much less to do so significantly.

As a counter, consider the example of the veteran

teacher of geometry who, retrospectively, acknowledges that for lo these many years of her career, she always worked especially hard to see that the male students learned the subject, for she always thought of the subject as preparation for basically male professions. Even though not always consciously, her habit was to devote more time and energy to individually helping the male students acquire the skills and understandings of geometry. Now, as an advocate of equal intellectual development for males and females, she wishes to alter her ingrained teaching habits. The mere desire to change those well-established habits may well not do the job. If, though, she were carefully to design and obligate herself to a policy according to which she must somehow monitor her expenditure of pedagogic time and effort according to the sex of her students, then her purpose of bringing about and maintaining a state of affairs in which her teaching behavior is no longer sexist might be achieved.

The point here is that the distribution of educational benefits within the classroom is within the teacher's power and authority and that the intraclassroom distribution can be nontrivial. A second point might be added. A group need not be legally classified as a suspect class for the teacher to treat that group of potential educational benefactors differently than another. That is, there are many ways in which a teacher might distribute educational benefits for not legal but pedagogic reasons. A child who especially enjoys mathematics, for example, might be allowed instruction with which he or she might progress well beyond the level of the other students in mathematics as a reward for putting extra effort into acquiring the content of a social science course. It appears that there would be occasions for a teacher's developing distributional policies as a guide to the systematic, fair, and pedagogically sound conduct of education. That the overall distribution of educational benefits across groups cannot be affected by an innermost distribution is, then, no reason to deny that there can be justifiable purposes for the teacher's establishing distributional policies.

THE PUBLICS OF EDUCATIONAL POLICIES

The third policy condition that was established in chapter 1 stated that the authorizing agent must undertake an obligation *for the purpose* of effecting some specified state of affairs (S) and to do so without violating any restrictive rules (R) by which the authorizing agent would claim to abide. As we come from having considered the nature of the *purposes* of educational policies, let us turn now to a consideration of another logically necessary feature of policy, the relevant public. (Recall the fourth policy condition.)

What descriptively might be said about the nature of the relevant publics of educational policies? More specifically, who constitutes the publics to whom revision of educational policies must be announced and whose views must be given due consideration if the policy is not to be violated in its revision? Unlike the purpose of educational policies, the relevant publics do not seem to vary with the category of policy. That is, the relevant publics of educational policies depend not upon whether the policies under consideration are curricular, methodological, resource, or institutional policies. Rather, the public to whom the policy must be announced depends upon where the policy is in the "nesting," and the public whose views must be given due consideration in the revision depends upon in what political and moral contexts the policy is located. Let us address the two publics in that order.

Where policy A is nested in policy B, one public of policy B consists of the policy-A authorizing agent. For example, if A is a teacher's curricular policy and B is the district curricular policy, for the authorizing agent of policy B to revise B without violating it, he must announce the revision to the authorizing agent of policy A. This can be shown to be so by pointing to the fact that it is the A-agent who can bring about conditions C and C' under which policy B obligates the B-agent to do X. To continue the same example, if policy B is such that the B-agent is obligated to approve of the teacher's curricular policies when they satisfy specified criteria, then the agent of policy A is the one who can bring about the conditions (here, when the criteria as specified by policy B are satisfied) under which the B-agent is obligated to do X (here, to approve of the curricular teaching policy). This "nesting" description of the public to which the revision must be announced is appropriate, though, only if the policy being revised is not the innermost policy in the nesting. If the policy to be revised is not B but A, and if there is no policy that is more inner than A, then the public to which the revision must be announced would have to be determined without reference to nesting, but with the more general description. Typically the public of the logically innermost or teaching policy would be the persons to whom the teaching is directed. For example, if a university professor of philosophy had a policy of allowing students independently to define substantive issues for their formal courses of study whenever the students demonstrated mastery of particular skills of philosophical analysis, it is the students who, by demonstrating mastery of those skills, can bring about the conditions that obligate the professor to take the particular action to which the policy obligates him.

Recall that the second public consists of that public whose views must, according to the political and moral context of the initial policy decision and its revision, be given due consideration. In the revising of a logically outermost educational policy in the context of a democratic political order, for example, the agent would have to give due consideration to the views of the citizens of that political order.

To illustrate the point, if the revision of a federal resource-allocation policy is in question, then the citizens' views regarding the order of federal enterprise priorities must be given due consideration for the policy to be revised without being violated. Or, if the policy is an innermost (teaching) methodological policy directed toward children, it might be that the public whose views should be taken into consideration would include the parents of those children, maybe other community members, and maybe the children themselves, depending on just who has a right to have his view taken into consideration within the given political system or moral order.[16] How the views should be collected and what would count as due consideration and whose views, in particular, are to be given consideration are matters addressed in chapter 4.

SUMMARY

At the outset of this chapter, it was found that the task of distinguishing an educational policy from just any policy presents a number of problems that, if not recognized, can lead to a faulty distinction. After demonstrating that it is a mistake to equate educational policies with policies of educational institutions and that it is potentially misleading to stipulate that educational policies are those policies that regard the educational programs of educational institutions, we considered the problem of how to develop a nonsubstantive theoretical description of educational policies. That task was accomplished by uncovering those categories of policies that are logically necessary to the systematic conduct of education, viz., curricular, methodological, re-

[16] For a consideration of what criteria the legal rights of children would have to satisfy to fulfill their moral rights under Rawls' theory of justice, see Victor L. Worsfold's paper, "A Philosophical Justification for Children's Rights," *Harvard Educational Review* 44, no. 1 (February 1974): 142–57.

source, and distributional policies. Further, it was noted that education policies commonly are "nested" one in another of the same category and that because of this relationship, educational policy decisions logically cannot be made in isolation. It was determined that policy A is nested in policy B when policy B limits or expands the range of admissible policy-A candidates, excepting when policy B prescribes in exact detail what person A is to do.

With these categories of educational policies, the notion of nesting and the types of policy purposes, we then considered the nature of the purposes of educational policies. In brief, while curricular and methodological policies of the outermost location in the nesting order appear to be achievable, the resource and distributional policies of that same nesting position are repeatedly achievable. On the other hand, all four categories of educational policy of the innermost nesting location are, in the systematic conduct of education, repeatedly achievable. Moreover, the S-purposes of the more outer policies may determine some R-purposes of the more inner policies. In that policies of the innermost and outermost nesting positions do not actually exist for all categories of educational policy, the point in discussing these logically possible classes of educational policies was not to describe the present conduct of education, but to suggest what sorts of policies would be required if education were to be conducted as systematically as is logically possible. And finally we noted that the two publics of any educational policy can, for the most part, be determined, respectively, by the position of the policy in the nesting order and by the political and moral contexts in which the education is conducted.

THREE

THE POLICY DECISION AS RATIONAL CHOICE

THAT ANY POLICY DECISION must, by the very nature of policy, be rational can easily be shown. But what sort of rationality can and should be expected of policy decisions is a more complicated matter that requires closer consideration. This chapter tries to pinpoint what sort of rational choice one faces when attempting to make a policy decision, whether it be a decision to adopt or not to adopt a particular policy, a decision to adopt one policy rather than another, or a decision to keep or discard a particular policy. In order to identify the nature of rational choice in such policy decisions, we need first to review the senses in which a choice might be said to be rational.

SENSES OF RATIONALITY

Rational Choice as Choice with Reason

Sometimes, perhaps most often when puzzled by something that someone does, we ask that person, A, why he did X. If A says that he had no reason in mind at all for doing X and that he did X simply on an impulse or whim, we would say that A's doing X was not rational. Such might be the case if we were to ask A why he demanded a Follis rather than a Gitane bicycle when it was clear that A did not know the differing virtues of the two bicycles. And we would also say that A's buying any bicycle at all was not rational if A had no reason whatsoever in mind for buying a bicycle, but instead bought it on an impulse. If, on the other hand, A had a reason for selecting a Follis over a Gitane (e.g., because the Follis's seat felt more comfortable), then his choice would, at least in one sense, seem rational. Likewise, if A were to buy a bicycle because, say, he had never owned one and had always wanted one, A's decision to buy it would in a way be considered rational.

In each case, A's choice or decision would be considered rational in the sense that A had *some* reason in mind for making the choice that he did. The contrary of a rational choice of this sort would be a choice on impulse or whim— a choice that we might call a nonrational choice. It is in this sense of rational choice that every policy decision necessarily must be rational, in that one of the policy conditions (as developed in chapter 1) is that the agent must undertake the obligation to act in accord with the conditional imperative at least for the purpose of achieving *some* state of affairs S. That is, the agent's having some reason is necessary to the concept of policy, which is to say that a policy decision must by its very nature be rational in this first sense of rational choice, i.e., choice with reason.

Rational Choice as Intelligent Choice

The second sense of rational choice is to be juxtaposed with an illogical or, sometimes, irrational choice rather than with a nonrational choice as in the case of choice with reason. For example, take the case of A's being faced with the problem of getting to Paris as fast as possible. Let us assume that A wants to get to Paris as fast as possible and that A perceives his getting there as fast as possible as overriding all other considerations, such as cost and previous plans. Further, let us imagine that A sees two options: he could catch an afternoon nonstop flight or he could wait until morning and make a connection through London. If under these conditions and with no additional considerations A concluded that he ought to catch the morning flight, we would consider his choice to be not rational in the sense that it would be illogical in light of his premises. That is, if A were, in spite of his reasoning, to delay leaving until morning because he had in mind some "reason" which even he perceived as irrelevant (e.g., that there are many structural similarities between the French and English languages), we would deem his decision to be irrational. If, instead, A were to think at the time of his choice that his reason was relevant, then his choice would be rational both in the first sense (choice with reason) and in the second. If, though, A were to think that his "reasons" do not count as reasons at all even though they still somehow function as the basis of his decision, then his choice would qualify as rational in neither sense. That is, it would be both nonrational and irrational.

A second case in which A's decision might be said to be irrational would be if A valued the achievement of state of affairs S_1 over S_2, if the achievement of S_2 were to preclude the achievement of S_1, ceteris paribus, and if A were in spite of these facts to choose to try to achieve S_2 instead of S_1. That is, either to choose less than the best perceived means for achieving given purposes or to choose to work contrary to one's purposes is to choose irrationally. Correlatively, to choose the best perceived means or to choose to promote one's purposes [1] is to choose rationally in the sense of choosing intelligently, i.e., choosing what logically follows from one's premises and with reference to what one perceives as relevant reasons. While a policy decision is necessarily rational in the first sense (choice with reason), it is clearly not necessarily rational in the second sense (intelligent choice), however desirable it be that we make intelligent policy choices.

Rational Choice as Choice with Method

The third sense in which a choice may be rational is what I shall call the method sense, or choice with method. One makes a rational choice in this method sense if the choice is made by appeal to some generalized decision procedure. Unlike choice with reason under which the choice is made for just any reason or reasons, choice with method is made under the dictates of a generalized decision tool. A paradigmatic case of such a decision tool is presented by Professor Batty in a Donald Duck comic book: "Why worry? Let flipism solve your problem! Life holds no terrors when you have embraced the philosophy of flipism! At every crossroad of life, let flipism chart your course!" [2] Professor Batty refers, of course, to the method of deciding between alternatives by the flip of a coin. Similar decision procedures would be always following another person's advice, always waiting for "things to work themselves out," and a host of historical

---

[1] All the necessary qualifiers are assumed, e.g., that the agent perceives no threat of harm or other intolerable barrier to choosing the best perceived means and to choosing to promote his purposes.

[2] *Walt Disney's Comics and Stories* 13, no. 5 (February 1953): 1.

examples such as the Roman auspex's making choices by checking the flight of birds and the haruspex's looking at entrails.

For purposes of developing an exemplar, a case of flipism will suffice. Imagine that a school principal has made a policy under which he personally will evaluate each teacher's teaching rather than delegate the task to the vice-principal, the only alternative the principal perceives. When asked why he chose the former, he responds, "Because it came up heads." Further, he adds that whenever he must decide whether he should take responsibility for doing something or delegate that task to his vice-principal, he always flips a coin, because he finds that he otherwise spends far too much time in trying to think through such decisions. Or, his reason could have been that he worries too much when he lingers over such decisions or that he suffers from the terror of deciding, to which Professor Batty alluded. Whatever the case, he decided by using a decision procedure that he chose with reason. (To my mind it is unclear whether we would label "rational" a choice that was made according to some decision procedure chosen on whim or impulse, i.e., without reason.) Now, while choice with method is not logically necessary to a policy decision, it is fairly common to find policy decisions made by using a method or decision procedure that has been chosen with reason. PPBS, POSDCORB, cost-benefit analysis, disjointed incrementalism, force-field analysis, simple majority voting, and polling are a few of seemingly innumerable examples.

WEAK AND STRONG SENSE RATIONALITY

At this point two things seem clear. First, all policy decisions are necessarily rational in the first sense: choice with reason. Second, not just any rational policy decision, even if rational in all three senses, would seem to be necessarily rational enough for an educational or any other public or policy decision. That is, one can imagine cases in which a choice might be made not only with reason, but also intelligently relative to the agent's perceived options and perhaps also according to a method which was chosen with reason and still fall short of being rational to an acceptable degree.

To identify more specifically how a policy decision made both intelligently and with a method chosen with reason might fall short of desirable rationality, it may be helpful to look at a hypothetical case that seems rational, but not rational enough. Imagine the following: a teacher who is responsible for deciding which students should be diverted into remedial-reading instruction and which should be allowed to continue in the main reading program chooses to make the decisions by flipping a coin because he does not really know how else one could choose and so that method frees him of the felt agonies of indecision. In this case the teacher's choice is rational in all three senses: (1) his choices are made with reason—the reason being that he wants to fulfill his responsibility for placing the students or, more simply, that by choosing he places the students and placement of the students is the goal he has in mind; (2) he perceives his choice to be the best of perceived alternatives in that it is made in accord with the method he has chosen—a method which happens to allow but one "alternative"; (3) his choice is made with a method which, in turn, he chose for the reason that it would free him of the agony of indecision. Although rational in all three senses of rational choice, the teacher's choice would not satisfy most of us as being "rational enough." In such a characterization of his choice, the suggestion is that the choice does not meet further normative criteria of rationality. Otherwise put, while his choice is rational, it so qualifies in but a weak sense and not in a more desirable, stronger sense.

In an attempt to uncover the additional criteria that

distinguish stronger sense from weaker sense rationality, let us return to the teacher who is responsible for deciding which students should be given remedial instruction. But this time, imagine that his choice is such that it would seem to be more rational than before. In this case his reason for choosing particular students for remedial instruction is not simply to place some in that class of students, but to place only those students under remedial-reading instruction for whom such instruction would, in his perception, be more beneficial than the relatively more advanced instructional program. Further, each of his choices is based on a consideration of reader-specific factors, such as the magnitude of their respective reading problems, which are in his view relevant to a decision of which program would be more educationally beneficial for the particular reader under consideration. Moreover, the method of using an examination cutoff score for making the decision was chosen not for just any reason, such as to free him from the agony of indecision, but for the perceived effectiveness of the method as a tool for discriminating between those students who would benefit more from the remedial program and those who would benefit more from the standard course of instruction.

I think it would be agreed that in the second case the teacher's choice seems more rational than in the first case. How, it should be asked, might we account for that fact? In responding to this question we can begin to see what more than simple rationality we typically demand of policy decisions. The first telling difference is, I think, to be found in what is allowed as an overriding reason for choosing at all. In the first case, the teacher's reason for deciding that some students rather than others were to be transferred to remedial instruction was merely to place some students in the remedial program. In the second case, the teacher's reason for making a choice was also to place some students in the remedial program, but this time with the qualification that only those students who could benefit more from the remedial rather than the standard instruction should be so placed. Now if we assume in both cases, as seems plausible, that the teacher has as a goal the appropriate placement of students, then in the second case the choice seems more rational because the teacher's reason for choosing makes reference to a more complete description of the particular goal or goals that he is trying to achieve in making the choice or choices.

Lest it not seem plausible that one might have in mind a fuller goal description than that to which his reasons for a choice make reference, I hasten to relate an actual rather than hypothetical case. A sixth-grade mathematics teacher once told me that he had adopted an "individualized method" of instruction to the end of enabling each student to go at his own pace *and* to waste less time in nonlearning activities, such as in waiting for the "slower" students to catch up. On later observing the teacher, I noted that his method consisted in having each child do a problem in a workbook, after which the child was to queue up at the teacher's desk to have the solution checked for correctness. The teacher's reason for checking the students' work individually was to enable students to work at their own respective paces. It had, I learned, not occurred to the teacher that each student was standing in the queue for more than half of the class time. Had the teacher's reason for the particular choice made reference to the more complete description of his goal, which included enabling students to waste less time in nonlearning activities, one suspects that the teacher would have chosen otherwise. But the point here is not to conjecture what might in fact correct poor teaching procedures. Rather, the point is a conceptual one: *if the agent's reasons for a particular choice make reference to a more complete description of the goal toward an achievement of which the agent intends his choice to con-*

*tribute, then the agent's choice is more rational than if his
reason makes reference to a less complete description of the
goal or goals.*

While this difference between the two cases may be
sufficient to account for the second choice seeming to be
more rational than the first, there are, I think, two other
differences that might be sufficient to account for some
variation in degree of rationality. Recall that in the first
case the teacher chose to place students in the remedial or
standard program without taking into account any facts
of the case under consideration. To make the decision he
appealed, instead, to a method without regard to the facts
of the case. That is, no matter whether the student could
breeze through Shakespeare or whether the student was
still stumbling through an elementary reading primer, the
student was placed in either the remedial or standard class,
depending upon what a flip of the coin dictated. In the second case, however, in making the choice of where to place
the student, the teacher took into account facts of the situation that he thought of as relevant. If one were to think of
how the coin landed as being a fact of the situation, then
the difference could be restated thus: in the second case
the teacher took into account facts of the situation that he
believed to be relevant on the grounds that they could in
some way affect the achievement or nonachievement of his
goals. Restated in this way, how the coin lands would not
count.

In terms of the analysis of 'policy' in chapter 1, this
difference between the degrees of rationality of the two
cases might more instructively be put in yet another way.
In order to have a policy, one must decide to do something
(X) whenever particular conditions (C) obtain, to the end
of achieving some goal or state of affairs (S). In the second
case the teacher believed his X-ing (in part, his attending

to the situation factors that he perceived as being likely to affect the achievement of (S), whenever faced with a placement decision (C), was likely to contribute to the goal of proper placement. *In the more rational of the two choices, then, the agent took into account situation factors that he believed to be relevant on the grounds that they affect the achievement or nonachievement of his goals.*

Though the second difference between the two cases, as the first difference, would also be sufficient to account for the second case's seeming to be the more rational of the two, there remains yet another significant difference. This remaining difference regards the choice of method that the teacher used in coming to his decision.

Recall that in the first case the teacher chose the method on the grounds that he believed that that method, flipism, would effectively free him from the agony of indecision. In the second case, on the other hand, he chose the method of deciding by using a particular examination cutoff score on the grounds that he believed that this method would prove effective for discriminating which students would benefit more from which program and so tell him which choice would be more likely to contribute to the achievement of his goal. In both cases the method was selected for its presumed effectiveness in leading to a choice that would promote the achievement of a goal (relief from agony and proper placement, respectively), but only in the second case do the grounds for selection of method make reference to the goal, i.e., proper placement, that provides the point of bothering to make such a choice at all. The goal of relief from indecision's agony is parasitic on the other goal and, as such, could not in a more rational decision serve as the sole or primary goal referent. That is, *in the more rational of the decisions, the agent used a decision method which he perceived to be an effective means for making a choice that he believed would contribute to the achievement of at least the goal that serves as the reason for making the choice at all.*

I suspect that this is the point that is behind the observation that bureaucratic choices are, by the very nature of institutions, generally only weakly rational: person A decides what ought to be achieved by person B and person B ignores what A had in mind and attends instead to "coping with the work situation," e.g., flipping a coin to avoid the agony of indecision. The problem is worth noting for whenever the authorizing agent (A_a) and the implementing agent (A_i) are different persons, as is commonly the case with institutional policies, the goal that provides the point of making particular choices and the goal for which the decision methods are chosen may become separated and so contribute to the making of less rational implementing choices.

Having identified three aspects in which a rational choice may be more or less rational, we are now in a position to suggest what would have to be true for a choice to be rational in the strongest imaginable, or ideal, sense. Let us address each aspect in turn. First, we can say that if an agent's choice is ideally rational, then it must be true that the agent's reasons for that particular choice make reference to a *complete* description of the goal toward an achievement of which the agent intends his choice to contribute.[3] Second, it must be true that the agent takes into account *all* situation factors that are deemed relevant on the grounds that they affect the achievement or nonachievement of the goal or goals. Third, it must be true that the agent's decision method is perceived by the agent as in fact an effective

[3] A complete description of the *goal* should not be confused with a description of all possible consequences of the policy action. All consequences include unintended effects as well as intended ones. Clearly, goals, when they are achieved, are *intended* consequences.

means for making his choice contribute to the achievement of at least the goal that serves as the reason for making the choice at all.

Two points in particular should be noted. One is that to arrive at these necessary criteria for an ideally rational choice, I have expunged not only the less-than-superlative elements, but also those unrestricted subjective elements that were previously allowed in the agent's perceptions and beliefs. For example, if a choice is to qualify as ideally rational, I think that we must require in the third point that the means be effective not only in the agent's perception, but also in actual fact—a matter that is not determinable until after the choice. Further, in the second point, it should be noted that indeed the capability of human knowledge is outstripped in that the ideally rational choice would require that all relevant situation factors be known. Even if they were all known, we would not have the means to know that fact. If they are not all known, then the choice cannot be rational in the ideal sense. It would appear, then, that only the first point presents no special problems, for the agent has only to have a reason that makes reference to a complete description of his own goal or goals. Such would seem clearly to be logically possible. However, it may not be psychologically possible. If goals of a choice can be both conscious and unconscious, and if, further, we do not have access to unconscious goals, then it must be that we cannot give reasons that make reference to a complete description of our goal or goals, for given the nature of the mind, we cannot know what all those goals are.

Perhaps all I have shown here is that ideal things are indeed, as discussed in chapter 1, ideal—in principle they cannot be achieved. The point of characterizing the ideal is not to identify what it is that we should want to achieve, but what we should want to approach as closely as possible. The best means, as the story of Western thought goes, for approaching the ideal are the canons of criticism, logical and scientific. For example, it is commonly accepted in the Western world that the way to find a decision procedure that approaches the most effective means for making choices that contribute to goal achievement is by scientific inquiry. In sum, then, at least in Western thought the normatively most rational choice possible is the one that at least is based on the qualitatively most scientifically held beliefs.[4]

If in our normative concept of rationality the epitome of rational choice is the thoroughly scientific choice, it would seem to follow that the more we collectively advance our scientific knowledge, the more rational our choices can be. But clearly accumulated scientific knowledge does not ensure even weakly rational choice. More to the point, I think, is the claim that the degree to which current scientific knowledge is brought to bear in policy decisions is a measure of the degree of rationality of choice of policy. But even that statement is potentially misleading, for there are cases in which to take the time to "bring the scientific knowledge to bear" is to fail to be rational. If, for example, a bear is charging a backpacker, for the backpacker to take the time to try to figure out, given what he knows (presume here that he knows everything about the situation that one would need to know to do the calculation), whether his chances would be better if he were to do battle with his staff, which is already in hand, or if he were to spend precious seconds in trying to free his gun, a more effective weapon, which is secured to his backpack. Even if the backpacker knows enough to figure out which option would give

---

[4] For one brief but engaging discussion of the early development of scientific inquiry as the most rational means for making choices, see Marx W. Wartofsky, "From Common Sense to Science: The Remarkable Greeks and the Origins of Criticism," in his *Conceptual Foundations of Scientific Thought* (New York: Macmillan, 1968).

him the better chance, it may well be that the seconds that his calculations would consume might be far too expensive to be acceptable, e.g., the bear might devour our super-scientific backpacker in mid-thought.

Now, though the policy maker does not typically have to make policy decisions with the threat of a charging bear, he often has to make them with time and dollar constraints. The teacher, for example, who is trying to decide on curricular policies for the coming academic year typically has very little time and no money to make the decisions. For the backpacker or the educator to hold out for the most rational choice in light of current scientific knowledge would surely not be rational. Or, in that time and dollar and other constraints might be viewed as contextual factors that are inexorably a part of every rational policy decision, it might be said that to give highest priority to trying to approach ideal rationality in every policy decision is not itself rational. In other words, an ideally rational choice is not necessarily the most rational policy choice, for policy choices most often must be made in situations and contexts which are less than ideal for "bringing to bear all that we know." In order to determine, then, what would constitute a rational policy decision, we must identify the conditions under which policy decisions have to be made, if they are to be made at all. That is, we need to uncover what concept of ideal rational choice is appropriate to policy decisions. To do that, we need first to get clear on just what sort of choice the policy decision is.

KNOWLEDGE CONDITIONS FOR
RATIONAL POLICY CHOICES

Since the point of even having any policy is to effect some state of affairs, S, that goal state must be a part of any description of any policy choice. As well, whenever the agent has any other purposes in mind which restrict the manner in which he is to try to achieve S, then those restrictive or R-purposes would have also to be a part of the description of his choice of policy. This section, though, is limited to an explicit consideration of the agent's S-purposes. To include the agent's R-purposes in a description would require our adding a somewhat cumbersome qualifier to each knowledge condition—a qualifier that would have to be placed on the perceived available means so as to allow only those means that serve the R-purposes. In other words, for convenience it will be helpful first to describe what one is doing when making a policy choice, next to indicate how the R-purposes restrict the choice, and then temporarily to abandon an explicit consideration of R-purposes.[5]

In skeletal form, whenever the agent is choosing a policy he is deciding upon a means for achieving a particular state of affairs, where doing a specified something whenever specified conditions obtain counts as a means. That is, the agent is trying to select a doing-conditions combination $(X\text{-}C)$ that will result in a state of affairs (S) he wants, for whatever the reason, to bring about. Now if the agent is trying to fulfill particular restrictive purposes as well, then his policy choice consists in selecting not just any effective doing-conditions combination $(X\text{-}C)$, but one that satisfies his R-purposes at the same time. For example, if a teacher wishes to effect a state of affairs in which a particular student knows how to spell "rhododendron" and if, at the same time, the teacher does not want to allow any means $(X\text{-}C)$ that counts as classical conditioning, then his choice would be limited to the perceived set of $X\text{-}C$ combinations that do not fall under a description of classical conditioning. More precisely, in choosing a policy, the agent

[5] When evaluating particular policies one would not, of course, be justified in abandoning consideration of the R-purposes.

is looking for an *X-C* means that (1) is such that it will or is likely to effect *S* and (2) does not fall under the set of *X-C* means that any *R*-purpose disallows. For purposes of simplicity, the latter feature of choosing a policy is not included in this section.

There are two kinds of sets of knowledge conditions under which policy choices are made: *game* conditions, the topic of game theory and much of decision theory, and what I shall call *nongame* conditions. Under game conditions, all outcomes (including *S*) of doing some *X* when some conditions *C* obtain are well specified; the agent not only knows which outcome he wants (*S*), but also can rank-order by his preference all outcomes that can be obtained by all means (*X-C*); all variables (*X-C* factors and combinations) which control outcomes (including *S*) are well specified; and there may be only a finite number of means (*X-C*) to achieve any possible outcome, including *S*.[6] Under nongame conditions, all outcomes of *X-C* are not necessarily well specified; the agent may not be able to rank-order all possible outcomes; all variables (*X-C* factors and combinations) which control outcomes are not necessarily well specified; and there is always, at least in theory, an infinite number of *X-C* means to achieve *S*. Although, as should become clear, most policy decisions are most commonly made under nongame knowledge conditions (types of conditions 4 and 5 below), there are two reasons to include game conditions (types of conditions 1–3 below) in this discussion. The first reason is that policies logically can be made under game conditions and, in fact, sometimes are. Second, a specification of policy choice under game conditions as an ideal model can be heuristically use-

---

[6] For a fuller yet brief discussion of the assumptions of game theory, see R. Duncan Luce and Howard Raiffa, *Games and Decisions* (New York: John Wiley & Sons, 1957), pp. 3–6.

ful to the policy maker, much as Boyle's law can be a useful model of behavior of gases, even though gases never actually behave in that way.

Knowledge Conditions 1: Choice under Certainty

The phrase 'decision under certainty' is borrowed from game theory and should not be confounded with 'certainty' as it is sometimes used in the literature of epistemology. When one makes a choice under certainty, he knows that if he does X whenever conditions C obtain, then state of affairs S will result. That is, he knows that X-C is a sure means for effecting S or, in other words, that the probability of S's resulting from X-C is 1. It should be noted that in a policy choice under certainty the agent *can* be mistaken. The sense in which his choice is made with certainty is this. There is a very strong reason to believe that if one chooses means X-C, then S will result. For example, if one has a thousand times dropped a chicken egg from the thirty-second story of a building when leaning out over a concrete sidewalk, and if the egg has broken on impact *every* time, and if all other experimenters had the same results, then the agent would know with certainty (in the sense of certain probability) that his X-C means will bring about S. That is to say, a choice under certainty does *not* mean that it is one which can be known to be correct by reference to language alone, i.e., a statement of choice under certainty is not known to be correct because it is analytic or tautological. Instead, a policy choice under certainty is one made with the knowledge of certain probability.[7] Note that on the $n + 1$ try, the egg might bounce back from the

---

[7] Certain probability is one of the six senses of certainty that C. I. Lewis distinguished. For his treatment of certain probability, see "The Empirical and the Probable," in his *Mind and the World Order* (New York: Dover, 1956), esp. pp. 330–31.

pavement into the hands of the experimenter. That is, that the agent makes a choice under certainty does not mean that S will always result from X-C. Instead, it means that the agent knows as an empirical fact that X-C has invariably been noted to lead to S.

While doubtless very few policy choices are made under such knowledge conditions, it might seem conceivable that such cases do occur. Consider the junior high teacher who quite by accident found that when he required that students present their homework papers as tickets for admission to class, the number of students who regularly did the homework increased significantly. If over time the teacher never saw a different effect and, on consultation with fellow teachers, found that they had made the same observation and if . . . (here one might wish to require that the teacher collect a sufficiently large and random sample), then we might say that the teacher's decision to adopt a policy of homework-as-ticket means for effecting a higher rate of homework submission was a choice under certainty. Though such a case might seem conceivable, it is, I think, unlikely that game conditions would actually occur outside the artificial bounds of games. All possible outcomes of X-C would have to be well specified. Given the present state of knowledge, that would not in fact seem possible. While a partial description of the teacher's goal would be to increase the homework-submission rate, a more complete description would also include, say, *not* getting the students to dread coming to class, which might be an unspecified outcome. My hunch is that one might actually be faced with policy choices under certainty only in the context of playing some sort of simple game in which there always exists at least one alternative that has a probability of 1 of resulting in a specified outcome. (Such a game, one suspects, would not be overwhelmingly interesting.)

Knowledge Conditions 2: Choice under Risk

The agent who makes a policy choice under risk does not know that S invariably results from X-C, but he does know the probabilities of each possible outcome. To consider an example that will conform to game conditions, let us take a choice for which the means and outcomes are well specified. The agent's job is to put the nth egg into the assembly of a good n-egg omelet.[8] He can select the nth egg either from the grade-A basket or from the grade-B basket. He knows from a random sample of grade-A eggs that the probability of grade-A eggs' being rotten is 0.008 and from a random sample of grade-B eggs that the probability of any grade-B egg's being rotten is 0.108. Thus he knows that the probability of his ending up with a good n-egg omelet is 0.992 if he selects an egg from the grade-A basket and 0.892 if he selects an egg from the grade-B basket. When faced with choice under risk, then, one makes the choice knowing that he may end up with a rotten omelet even if he makes the best perceived choice. This is *not,* though, to say that when the agent plays the probabilities correctly that he *always* selects the means that is *most* likely to result in S. In the omelet case, if the agent had thought of a third possibility, that of checking the nth egg by first breaking it into a dish by itself, his chances of ending up with a good n-egg omelet would have been improved. But again, it must be noted that a decision made under game conditions must assume that all allowable means (X-C) are well specified. Except, then, in the context of games, so defined, the X-C means for achieving the desired state of affairs S are not exhausted and do not have all probabilities defined. Yet, given that in any choice we

---

[8] The idea for this omelet example is borrowed from Luce and Raiffa, *Games and Decisions,* p. 227, but I have altered the details to fit my purposes.

are limited to those options we perceive, many more choices than fall under game conditions might seem to be choices under risk in the sense that we perceive them *as if* they were under game conditions.

Knowledge Conditions 3: Choice under Uncertainty

As in the case of the first two types of knowledge conditions, when one faces a policy choice under uncertainty, he knows all the possible outcomes, including S, for all the possible X-C combinations. But unlike the situation in choice under certainty (in which the probabilities are known to be 0 and 1) and in choice under risk in which the probabilities that S will result from any X-C are known, in choice under uncertainty the probabilities are unknown. To make an example of choice under uncertainty we need only to return to our omelet-maker's decision and delete his knowing the probabilities that grade-A and grade-B eggs, respectively, will be rotten. When faced with such a choice one is at a loss to know what to do. To decide on "gut feelings," hunches, whims, or the like would likely be thought as rational a way to decide as any. Notice that this is in contrast to choice under certainty and choice under risk where in either case the option with the higher probability would be considered the more rational choice.

One can create more complex examples than the omelet case of choice under uncertainty in which what counts as the more rational option might depend, curiously enough, upon whether the agent is a pessimist or an optimist. As illustration, think of a person who faces the following situation: [9] The agent is presented with two urns filled with metal balls of a uniform size. He is told that he may blindly draw for his keeping one of the balls from one of the urns. Further, he is informed (here assume honesty and correctness) that the urn on the left contains platinum and lead balls in a proportion not specified, while the right urn contains gold and silver balls, likewise in unspecified proportions. As in all game-conditions choices, the agent knows what outcome he prefers and can rank-order all possible outcomes, i.e., utilities are assigned. Let us say that the agent's preferences are such that he assigns them the following utilities: platinum, 1000; gold, 100; silver, 10; lead, 1. If he is a pessimist (i.e., if he assumes that the worst will happen), then to choose rationally he must apply the *maximin rule,* for he wants to maximize the minimum utility. Here, to be rational the pessimist would choose to select a ball from the right urn, so that he would at least draw a silver ball. If, on the other hand, the agent were an optimist (i.e., if he assumes that the best will happen) then to choose rationally he must apply the *maximax rule,* for he wants to maximize the maximum utility. Given the options and possible outcomes, to choose rationally the optimist must select a ball from the left urn so that he would at least have a chance of drawing a platinum ball. Having figured out the utilities and the nature of this problem, our agent might decide to establish a game-playing policy to the effect that whenever faced with such a game choice he would always choose (if he were as policy maker feeling optimistic) the option that offers the possibility of the outcome with the highest utility.

As with the two earlier game-conditions choices, the possibility that educational or other social or public policy choices could be made under game conditions seems slim. Yet, as before, many policy choices are in fact made *as if* they were made with uncertainty under game conditions. For example, take the parent who has heard that students who go to Rigorous School either drop out altogether or stick it out and are admitted to top-notch universities, and that students who go to Mediocre School all make it through high school, though none is subsequently admitted to the best universities. If, in this parent's perception, all possible outcomes are so specified and if he assigns each outcome utilities, he may, without acknowledging the host of other possible outcomes, conditions (relevant factors), and actions, choose to send his child to Rigorous School (if he is optimistic) or to Mediocre School (if he is pessimistic). It might be noted, as intimated earlier, that to make a choice as if game conditions obtain when one knows that game conditions do not obtain would not necessarily seem to be to choose rationally. Rather, it would be to choose in an inappropriate fashion or with the unfulfillable wish that the choice were simpler so as to be soluble by application of one of game theory's mathematical models.

Knowledge Conditions 4: Choice under Partial Ignorance [10]

Under the nongame conditions of choice under partial ignorance, the agent in some sense knows (here perhaps "makes statistical inference") that S will result if he does X whenever conditions C obtain, but he does not know all the outcomes of doing X-C. Stories of persons being granted three wishes frequently garner the moral from the fact that when the person decides what to wish, he does so under partial ignorance.[11]

Smith, an unemployed English miner, asked the good fairy for two hundred pounds; the next day the foreman at

[10] Though Luce and Raiffa, *Games and Decisions,* use the terms 'partial ignorance' and 'complete ignorance' (pp. 299–306 and 294–98, respectively), the way in which I employ them here is related to their use only in a very rough way.

[11] These three-wish stories, including the one that I present, commonly appear to be variations on an early twentieth-century horror story: W. W. Jacobs, "The Monkey's Paw," in *Modern Short Stories,* ed. Margaret Ashmun (New York: Macmillan, 1914).

the mine where Smith's son was employed brought Smith an envelope containing two hundred pounds as a gesture of sympathy from the owner of the mine, for Smith's son had that very morning perished in an accident at the mine. For a second wish Smith asked for his son back; the next day, hearing a knock at the door, Smith opened it and in floated the presence of Smith's son which made the house seem haunted, eerie, and most uncomfortable for Smith. For the third wish Smith asked the fairy to take away his son's presence; the fairy complied.

In the case of each wish, Smith knew that if he made a particular request (X) in the presence of the fairy (C) that what he requested would come true. What Smith did not know was what *all* the possible outcomes of X-C were. Now Smith, the astute observer might remark, could have avoided the occurrences of the other unspecified and unwanted outcomes by cleverly tacking a qualifier to each request, such as, "I wish for two hundred pounds under the condition that no other outcomes result which would not, in my view, be desirable." While it seems advisable to remember to attach such qualifiers when visited by a wish-granting fairy, there does not appear to exist such a neat way out of the problem of partial ignorance when faced with policy choices in a world in which just saying things usually does not make them so. In the "real world," one *cannot* know how X-C should be altered to make S obtain without any intolerable other outcomes *until* one knows what specifically the other likely outcomes of X-C are.

The evidence of choice under partial ignorance is frightfully common—common enough to suggest that it may be the knowledge condition under which both policy and nonpolicy choices have most commonly to be made. In the late 1960s do-your-own-thing curricular policies were introduced into many schools, so that students would be less "uptight." Indeed (maybe) students became less uptight as a result; but reading, writing, and computational skills suffered. So the conjecture goes. But in the conjecture partial ignorance of a second sort might be at play. All the variables that control outcomes are typically not known. So a policy that effects S in one context may not, to our surprise and chagrin, do so in another. In such a case of partial ignorance, though the agent knows that if he does X whenever C, then S results, he may not know the critical features of the X-C combination. That is, even though the X-C combination that results in S and other outcomes is not precisely specified, it is roughly specified. The two sorts of partial ignorance, respectively, occur: (1) when the agent knows what well-specified X-C will likely result in S, but does not know what outcomes other than S will result; and (2) when the agent knows only that a roughly specified X-C generally results in S and does not know what outcomes other than S are likely to result.

For policy choices there is a third sort of factor that, if unknown, would increase the level of ignorance, viz., whether conditions C will occur with sufficient frequency for S to be achieved by doing X whenever C obtains. For illustration, suppose that a teacher has a goal of getting tenth graders to learn a prescribed geometry curriculum. From past teaching experience he knows that those learnings can result from his limiting his instruction to responding to student-initiated questions. That is, he has good reason to believe that his X-C means (responding whenever students initiate questions) is generally effective in achieving the goal. Imagine that this geometry teacher transfers to another school and, further, allow that it is still true that his means is effective in achieving the goal, *but only,* of course, if the policy conditions C (here, students initiating questions) recur with sufficient frequency. Unbeknownst to our geometry teacher, it may also be the case that his new students are too shy to initiate questions or that the culture

discourages it or that the prevailing teacher-tells-all methodology of the school has taught students not to take the
initiative. That is, while he may know that doing X whenever C obtains will contribute to S, he may not know that C
will recur frequently enough to achieve S. In such a case,
the teacher's methodological policy must be made under a
third sort of partial ignorance. In short, under this kind of
partial ignorance, the means and outcomes may be well
specified, but it is not known whether the universe will
"cooperate" in bringing about the conditions with sufficient
frequency for the policy action to effect the desired state of
affairs.

Under partial ignorance, the most rational choice
would appear to be that which is based on the most informed guess the agent is able to make. That is, the most
rational choice would be the choice that brings to bear the
scientifically best available information—available to the
agent within the constraints of the particular policy choice
—by using the most sophisticated tools of inference that
the agent has at his disposal.

Knowledge Conditions 5: Choice under Complete Ignorance

An agent may be said to face a choice under knowledge conditions of complete ignorance if he does not know
what means (X-C) will effect the state of affairs (S) that
he desires to bring about, nor does he know other outcomes
of X-C candidates that might occur to him. He knows only
what state of affairs he would like to see eventuate, but he
has no more than "gut feelings" or wild guesses about
specifically what X-C might effect S. If for some reason the
agent nonetheless must choose some policy, e.g., he has
been directed by his superior in rank to "take care of that
problem" or he has received funds for immediate implementation of some policy to bring about S, then he must

make that choice under complete ignorance.[12] Though it does not seem rational to await a sound choice from conditions of complete ignorance, it might seem rational for him to "do just something" or to "try just anything," if some choice must be made. Even such crisis and desperation moves may strike us as quite rational when there is nothing much to lose, such as when the patient is terminally ill anyhow. But when there is much at stake, to refuse to make any policy or to refuse to take any sort of deliberate action may be as rational as anything, especially when the delay of the policy choice is used to gain time for altering the knowledge conditions from complete ignorance to partial ignorance. Indeed, the most rational policy choice under complete ignorance would generally appear to be to table the choice pending further study.

To summarize the logically distinct knowledge conditions under which policy might be made, there are two general categories into which all knowledge conditions fall: game conditions and nongame conditions. There are, further, three types of game conditions: choice under certainty, choice under risk, and choice under uncertainty.

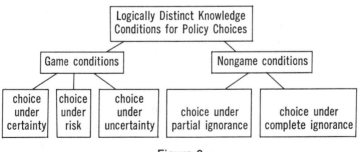

Figure 3

<hr>

[12] I grant that it may seem odd to call a wild, blind guess a choice. Faced with such a predicament, one might say, "I understand that I am expected to choose a policy, but I don't see what that choice might be."

The two types of nongame conditions are choice under partial ignorance and choice under complete ignorance.

MODELS FOR RATIONAL POLICY CHOICE

Now we can, I think, conceive of a world in which social policies, including educational policies, might be made under game conditions. We have only to think of a world in which all goals are articulated and all the facts are "in." In such a world, not only would all goals be defined in complete detail, but also all outcomes of *all* possible actions would be well specified, as would be all variables which control each possible outcome. Because no value that might be needed for a mathematically defined decision would be unknown, all policy choices could be made rationally by appeal to the appropriate mathematical formula. In such a world, scientific methodology would be impossible, for there would be no hypothesis to propose. Knowledge in that world, including knowledge of what actions are effective, would perhaps be presented as theorems (if the facts of the world had been made so by definition) or as completely confirmed "theses" (if the facts had been established by perfectly comprehensive, absolutely complete and infallible inquiry). The only question marks that would remain would appear in those instances in which chance happened to be introduced systematically, by the arranging of situation elements in such ways as to allow particular outcomes to be unknown to the chooser in advance of the choice (e.g., requiring that someone blindly draw metal balls from urns).

But while we can conceive of a world in which all policies would be made under game conditions, the description does not seem to fit our world, nor does it fit our imaginable future if scientific inquiry remains the very best form of inquiry we shall ever have. As long as we hold to scientific methodology with its lack of mechanism for perfect confirmation of hypotheses, it shall always be the case (except, of course, under arbitrarily defined game conditions) *neither* that all the outcomes of any action can be specified *nor* that all the variables which control each possible outcome can be specified. So then, to treat any policy choice as a choice under game conditions would be to err in at least some ways. Correlatively, to approach any policy choice as if it were a choice under game conditions and, at the same time, to fail to acknowledge the sorts of mistakes that are inherent in using decision procedures that the knowledge conditions do not warrant, is to mistake a heuristically useful model for a set of instructions on how to deduce correct truth claims from a description of conditions that do not obtain.

Thus it appears that policy choices are made under nongame conditions and, further, that they are most commonly made under partial ignorance. In those cases in which a policy choice falls under conditions of complete ignorance, it would be considered rational to delay the choice for purposes of inquiry the point of which is to alter the knowledge conditions in such a way as to bring about conditions of partial ignorance.

So, then, we can say that in actuality social policy choices are made, rationally or not, under partial ignorance. Moreover, the policy choice based on stronger scientific evidence regarding the relative effectiveness of various means $(X-C)$ for achieving the goal state of affairs would generally be viewed as more rational than the policy choice which is based on weaker or no evidence. In the literature of policy analysis in particular and in that of planned action in general, there is no dispute over the point that to be rational a choice must at least include consideration of empirical evidence. The discussion arises, instead, over the question of what additionally must be true for the policy choice to count as rational; namely, what general description must the policy fit in order for the policy choice to count as rational? Under one view, only that policy option which would maximize specified utilities would be a rational choice. For example, if the policy maker were concerned with establishing curricular policies to encourage, say, aesthetic appreciation, other things being equal the only rational choice would be that one X-C which maximizes aesthetic appreciation. According to the second model, not the maximization of utilities, but the satisfaction of criteria that are deemed "good enough" is the guide to rational choice, where "good enough" may not be the best possible. Under the third view, a policy choice is more rational than any other if its ratio of benefits to costs is higher than the benefit/cost ratio of any of the considered alternatives.

In the policy literature, the first two of these models of rational policy choice are labeled, respectively, "maximizing" (or sometimes "optimizing" [13]) and "satisficing." The third, which has not to my knowledge been given a name, I shall entitle "contextual optimizing." Since the three models were developed roughly in that order and since the second, satisficing, was proffered as an improvement over the first, maximizing, and contextual optimizing as an improvement over satisficing, it will be helpful to give a fuller consideration to each in turn.

Maximizing

What is sometimes called the classical model of rational policy choice requires that the agent choose *the best* policy. Period. Commonsensically the model seems sound: only the best option would constitute a rational policy choice. The only qualification that may initially seem necessary would limit the choice to the *in fact* possible choices,

[13] For example, see C. West Churchman, *Prediction and Optimal Decision* (Englewood Cliffs, N.J.: Prentice-Hall, 1961).

rather than allowing the choice to range over all logically possible choices. The point, clearly, to such a qualifier would be that since not all logically possible choices are actually possible in this world, to choose the best of logically possible policies might be to choose a policy that could never, at least in the time and space of this world, serve its purpose. For example, one might determine that the best of logically possible policies for improving the reading levels of the population would be to utilize a technology that would restructure the brain of each fetus in such a way as to result in the child's being born with a high-level reading ability. By definition, the policy would be effective in achieving the desired state of affairs. In fact, lacking such technology, the proposed policy could not even be implemented, much less be effective. The best choices in pipe dreams, unfortunately or not, do not always seem to be actually the best choices.

To present a weaker formulation, but a stronger case for the maximizing model, it should be said that a rational policy choice requires that the agent choose the best of policies that are factually possible. Once again, on a commonsensical glance the model seems sound, for surely to choose a policy rationally one is obligated to choose the best of factually possible policies. And once again, at first blush that does seem to be how those of us who choose rationally go about it.

But while the maximizing model of rational choice may seem phenomenologically correct, as a reconstruction of what is logically entailed in a rational choice it falls well short of the mark. For illustration, let us say that a group of reading specialists have somehow decided that over the long run the best policy for improving the reading levels of the population would be to give systematic language instruction beginning at the age of two. In order to have determined that such a policy would be the best policy, they would had to have identified a set of factually possible policies that would have included the best policy and then have selected that policy from the set, for without having identified such a set of factually possible policies they would be faced with a *very large* number of factual possibilities. For example, logically they could have chosen to begin instruction at exactly two years, or at two years and one second or two years and two seconds or two years and three seconds or. . . . Further, they could choose to give instruction for 10.0 minutes per day, for 10.1 minutes per day, for 10.2 minutes per day, or. . . . (Or, they might decide not to give instruction every day, but every other day or every week or not even periodically.) Further, they might choose to begin the period of instruction at 12:00 noon, at 12:01 P.M., at 12:02 P.M., at 12:03 P.M., and so forth. One could go on introducing possible variations in other factors (e.g., resources, content of instruction, distribution of instruction, methodology), each of which increases the number of factually possible alternative policies at a rate that would alarm any policy maker who takes seriously the maximizing model and who thus must consider all factually possible policies in order to determine that the set from which he chooses a policy contains the best possible policy. To review such a very large set of possible policies in order to determine that one had identified a set of options that includes *the* best policy would itself not be possible in fact, given time, energy, and resource limitations on policy making.

One might protest that in building this case against the maximizing model that I have reached the heights of plain silliness, for of course one need consider only those factors and variations that really matter. Whether, for example, instruction would begin at 12:00 or 12:01 clearly would not matter. But this objection serves only to shift the locus of the problem, for in order to determine what factors and variations really might affect the outcome and the efficiency of any factually possible policy, the reading specialists would have to sort through all those factors and permutations in order to come up with the criteria that would distinguish between those that really matter and those that do not. So again the policy maker would be faced with a number of considerations so large that ever to arrive at a rational choice, so defined, would not in fact be possible. Indeed the maximizing model, if taken seriously, would have the policy maker running in a logically inescapable circle: to make a rational policy choice he must choose a factually possible policy; but to determine some set of policy candidates from which he must choose, he must perform feats that are not in fact possible.

Satisficing

Even though the maximizing model is not logically tenable as a model for rational policy choice, something about it does seem to be on the right track. That is, one thing that would have to be true of any policy for it to seem a rational choice would be that it must be superlative in some sense, otherwise there would be no reason to choose it over the other alternatives. It is that element of the maximizing model that the satisficing model was proffered to save, without retaining the vicious circle. The central difference between the two models is this. While to choose rationally under the maximizing model one must choose *the* best policy or the policy which maximizes utilities, to choose rationally under the satisficing model one has only to choose some policy that is "good enough," where there might be quite a large number of policies that would qualify as good enough.[14] The change warrants a sigh of relief, for the

[14] Herbert A. Simon, *Models of Man* (New York: John Wiley & Sons, 1957), p. 205.

satisficing model seems at least to make rational choice actually possible. To put it another way, satisficing allows one actually to make a choice. The difficulty, as we shall see, consists in the fact that it allows a far greater range of choices than would be considered rational. That is, it allows rational choice and then some.

Care should be taken to note that the satisficing model was not initially proposed as an adequate model for rational policy choice. Instead, it was offered as a description of how people commonly make choices. Satisficing, then, was not proposed as a rational way to make policy choices, but as an empirical and psychological thesis regarding how people typically come to make particular decisions: "Most human decision making, whether individual or organizational is concerned with the discovery and selection of satisfactory alternatives; only in exceptional cases is it concerned with the discovery and selection of optimal alternatives." [15] In some instances the satisficing model is based on the biological thesis that "organisms adapt well enough to 'satisfice'; they do not, in general, 'optimize.'" [16] If satisficing were always presented as a phychological or biological thesis and not as a theoretical description of rational policy choice, then it would not be an appropriate topic for this discussion. In the policy literature, though, one finds satisficing treated as if it were a model for rational policy choice. [17] Therefore, it must be evaluated as such.

For an illustration of a policy choice made on the satisficing model, let us return to the case of the reading specialists who have decided to adopt some policy of giving systematic language instruction to two-year-olds. This time we need not require that the reading specialists choose the

[15] James G. March and Herbert A. Simon, *Organizations* (New York: John Wiley & Sons, 1958), pp. 140–41.

[16] Simon, *Models of Man*, p. 261.

[17] For example, see Charles E. Lindblom, *The Decision-Making Process* (Englewood Cliffs, N.J.: Prentice-Hall, 1968), p. 24.

best policy possible in fact. Instead we need only demand that they choose a policy that is good enough. Note that "good enough" suggests criteria in addition to the general goal of the policy to improve the reading levels of the population. The range of possible criteria candidates reaches to the ends of one's imagination: good enough to get the Congress to appropriate funds, good enough to satisfy the Union of Reading Specialists, good enough to muster community support, good enough to improve reading-test scores of fourth graders by two grade levels, and so on. According to the model, the policy maker need only require that his policy choice satisfy some such criterion to be rational. The rub comes thus: any criteria will do, *even* criteria that are not rational even to the policy maker himself, much less to the policy's relevant public. For example, a criterion might be irrational in the policy-maker's view and still good enough in that it might satisfy some unconscious psychological need, and so would fit the satisficing model for rational choice. Or, the criteria for "good enough" might be rational in the policy-maker's view, but not in the collective view of the relevant public, as might be the case if the specialists were to choose some policy designed, perversely, to increase reading difficulties so as to ensure a future need for their expertise in the solution of reading problems.

The satisficing model "goes wrong" in at least two ways. The first is that while it is purported to be a model for rational (strong sense) policy choice, it allows choices that are clearly not rational. The second is that if satisficing is to count as a model for rational choice, then it must at some point provide criteria for rational choice. According to the model, a rational choice is one that is good enough. So far, so good. But then the model fails to provide criteria that would distinguish *rational* "good enoughs." That is, the model says that whatever policy is good enough for the policy maker is, by definition, a rational policy choice. Though of course one can stipulate any meaning for any word and not be subject to criticism, to stipulate a nonstandard meaning and then to proceed to pretend that the nonstandard meaning is in fact standard is at best to fail to understand the standard concept. To my knowledge no one has tried to defend satisficing as an adequate model for rational policy choice. Those who recommend the model seem only to assume that it is defensible. But the fact that there are those who use the satisficing model without recognizing that the model is inadequate does not change the fact that it is an inadequate model for rational policy choice.

Contextual Optimizing

The difficulty with the maximizing model lies not in what it prescribes, but in its not allowing rational choice to be actually possible. The difficulty with satisficing, on the other hand, rests not with what it fails to allow (i.e., rational choice) but with what it does not disallow (i.e., irrational choice). To overcome these problems, we need a model that *both* admits the factual possibility of rational choice, lest the concept be lost, *and* disallows policy choice that generally, or at least in the view of the relevant public, would not be considered rational.

A solution can be found in providing a model that (1) limits the field of alternatives to be considered to a manageable number and (2) requires that the field of admissible choices include a choice which would be deemed rational by the relevant public of the policy. Put otherwise, we need a model which requires that the policy maker choose the policy which satisfies the relevant public's criteria for rational choice. Further, if the model assumes that rationality admits of degree, then it shall *not* have to require, as the maximizing model requires, that to be rational at all a policy choice must be the best factually possible policy. That is, if the model assumes that some policy choice might be less rational than another alternative that is not considered and yet be a rational choice, then the policy maker need choose only the best of the considered alternatives in order to make a rational choice. The construction of such a model might begin as follows: a rational policy choice is one for which the benefits outweigh the costs in the view of the relevant public, including the policy maker. Further, to choose policy candidate *A* is more rational than to choose policy candidate *B* if the policy-*A* benefit/cost ratio appears to be greater than that for policy *B*. In other words, given the *public context* of a policy, a policy choice is rational if, in the view of the relevant public, it has a higher or more *optimal* benefit/cost ratio than considered alternatives.[18]

As a beginning this formulation of contextual optimizing is, I think, promising in that it avoids the problems of maximizing and satisficing; but much remains to be done to explicate the model.[19] What, for example, is to constitute "the view of the relevant public"? That on which all persons in the public agree unanimously, or the view of the majority, or what? In that the model suggests that

[18] Contextual optimizing should not be understood as just any cost-benefit analysis. Not infrequently, cost-benefit analysis is employed as if game conditions obtained when in fact they do not and costs are calculated in dollars only. The model of *contextual* optimizing can correctly be used only if the policy agent recognizes that nongame conditions of partial ignorance obtain and if costs and benefits are not limited to monetary terms.

[19] For presentations of similar models that are offered as ways out of the difficulties of maximizing and satisficing, see Donna H. Kerr, "When Is an Educational Policy a Good Policy?," *Studies in Philosophy and Education* 8, no. 4 (Fall 1974): 258–77; and Alex C. Michalos, "Rationality Between the Maximizers and the Satisficers," *Policy Sciences* 4, no. 2 (June 1973): 229–44.

what counts as a rational policy choice boils down to a question of some sort of collective rationality (the topic of the next section), in order to explicate contextual optimizing it is necessary to decide what sorts of ingredients are necessary for a group or collective choice to count as rational. And clearly not just any "sway of the mass" will do, in that the model requires that the choice be *judged* rational in the view of the relevant public. (Here it is again perhaps appropriate to note that while personal policies might have no public beyond the policy maker himself, social or public policies, such as educational policies which provide the focus for this book, unavoidably have relevant publics beyond the agent of the policy.) My conceptual point is that even if a single agent in solitary deliberation actually decides a public policy, for that policy to be rational (i.e., acceptable on rational grounds), it must be rational in the view of the relevant public.

A second point that needs attention and that frequently goes unnoticed, as it seems to hide behind the label "benefit/cost ratio" or "cost-benefit analysis," regards the content of "benefit" and "cost." What should count as a benefit? a cost? That is, what sorts of benefits and costs should be considered relevant to a policy choice? Clearly, a shift in view as to what should count as a benefit or cost can mean a shift in view as to what policy choice is rational. And when one has decided what factors are relevant to a policy choice, then a second problem appears: what weight should be given each sort of benefit and cost? Should, for example, an economic benefit be weighted more or less heavily than a psychological or political or legal or moral benefit? Or, should a benefit to one group count more than a benefit to another? If indeed a calculation of the benefit/cost ratio is necessary to a rational policy choice and if such a calculation requires assignment of values and appeal to norms, then what constitutes a rational policy choice is inextricably a normative question. It is to such normative questions as are necessary to any full explication of rational policy choice that we turn in chapter 4.

RATIONALITY IN COLLECTIVE CHOICE

The work that has been done on rational choice under game conditions addresses the question of how a person would have to choose if he were to take into account only his own interests as an individual. That is, game theory focuses on rational choice where the goal is the satisfaction of an individual's own wishes as an individual. Now, if it is the case that to be rational a policy choice must be rational not only in the view of the policy maker, but also in the view of the relevant public, then discussions of rationality in game choices can throw little light on the collective rationality of policy choices. The question to which we need an answer is what must be true to say that a policy choice is rational in the view of the relevant public. Until we have an answer we shall not know what must be true to say that a policy choice is rational. The plan of this section is to begin with what would seem to be the strong-sense formulation of 'rational in the view of the relevant public' and then to outline the modifications that have been offered to avoid the difficulties of this strong-sense thesis.

The strongest interpretation would, I think, be as follows: rational public policy choice entails that *each* individual in the relevant public view the choice as rational. Let us call this the thesis of *distributive rationality*. On the other end of the continuum, one might define "rational in the view of the relevant public" as "rational enough" to those individuals of the relevant public whose views "matter," where some sort of restrictive criteria would have to be established for 'rational enough' and for 'individuals whose views matter.' This might be called the thesis of *preferential rationality.* I suppose that one might identify as the extreme that preferential rationality in which the choice need be rational to but one individual of the relevant public. Now it might be objected that by calling distributive rationality the stronger interpretation and preferential rationality the weaker reading I am carting in a preference for democracy over, say, dictatorship. While I would not wish to deny that such is my preference, the objection is not warranted. My point is not normative but logical: if a choice is distributively rational, then it is necessarily rational to every individual, no matter what the description of the situation; when a policy choice is preferentially rational, it is necessarily rational only to those persons who, under a specified normative description, are to receive preferential treatment. By "stronger interpretation," then, I mean that interpretation which would necessarily specify a rational policy choice under a greater number of substantive descriptions.

Our initial question is, then, whether a rational policy choice is in fact possible if we require that the choice be rational to each individual. One often hears the popular response to the question: "Sure it would be rational if everyone agreed that it is rational, but in fact all persons in any group rarely agree on anything!" That is, while the logical point is conceded, the factual point is disputed. Or, more specifically, the popular response says that within any group, as the interests of individuals differ, what they individually consider to be rational differs. While the claim seems correct, it misses the point. The question is *not* whether any choice that one individual deems rational would be viewed as rational by every other individual in the group; rather, it is whether in the case of any particular policy decision there exists some alternative which would be viewed as rational by every individual in the group. If such an alternative does exist, then a distributively rational policy choice is in fact possible.

One response to this question can be found in Vilfredo Pareto's discussion of the maximization of utilities in the context of economics. In summary form, the suggestion of Pareto is that a distributively rational policy option exists whenever there is a factually possible policy option in which it is possible to increase the benefit/cost ratio of any one individual without decreasing that of another individual. When a state of affairs in which such an increase is impossible has been achieved, then the maintenance of the status quo is the rational collective choice, in that the "maximum of ophelimity" (or, more popularly, the "maximum of optimality") has been reached.[20] That is, a policy choice is distributively rational when it is Pareto optimal, and a policy choice is Pareto optimal when it will make at least one individual better off without making any other worse off.

To exemplify a Pareto-optimal policy choice, imagine that in one of the states in the Union there are two perceived policy options for financing public schools. One is that school dollars continue to be raised by a system of local levies; the other is that monies be collected, instead, through a state income tax. If there are n persons who are citizens of the state and if all those persons count as part of the relevant public, then there would be 2^n possible patterns of preference or, here, rational views of the options. For convenience of illustration, let us say that in-

[20] For further discussion of Pareto optimality (ophelimity) and Pareto-optimal choices, see Talcott Parsons, *The Structure of Social Action* (New York: Free Press, 1968), 1:242–49; and Maurice Allais's and Talcott Parsons's entries on Pareto in the *International Encyclopedia of the Social Sciences,* ed. David L. Sills (New York: Macmillan & Free Press, 1968), vol. 11, esp. pp. 403–7 and 413–14, respectively.

stead of three million, only three persons constitute the relevant public. There would, then, be eight (2^3) logically possible patterns of rational views:

	Person A	Person B	Person C
(1)	levy	levy	levy
(2)	levy	levy	tax
(3)	levy	tax	levy
(4)	tax	levy	levy
(5)	levy	tax	tax
(6)	tax	levy	tax
(7)	tax	tax	levy
(8)	tax	tax	tax

This is to say that logically there would be two distributively rational or Pareto-optimal policy choices, (1) and (8). And if we had worked through $2^{3,000,000}$ preference patterns, there would still logically be but two distributively rational policy choices: in the one in which the ratio of benefit/cost would be higher for *every* citizen if the local levy system were maintained and in the one in which the benefit/cost ratio would be higher for *every* citizen if a state income tax were introduced.

In asking whether a distributively rational policy choice is in fact possible, in Pareto's terms we are asking whether a Pareto-optimal policy choice exists. The answer is yes, but if and only if it is the case that either all citizens find the levy more rational than the tax or all citizens think the tax is rationally preferable to the levy. Now it might appear as if we are back to the popular response to our question, "Sure it would be rational if everyone agreed that it is rational, but in fact all persons in any group rarely agree on anything!" But we may have gained some heuristic ground if we take the view that distributive rationality under Pareto's description makes it clear that there are always two logically possible patterns of agreement. If we now add to that the observation that there is always a *very large* number of factually possible policy options, then might it not be possible to adjust and readjust the proposed policy options until such point as we find a Pareto-optimal policy choice. For example, we could tinker with the local levy and state tax alternatives until such point as the benefit/cost ratio for, say, the levy would be higher for *everyone*.[21] Under this view, distributive rationality is possible if someone is ingenious enough to figure out how to alter the policy alternatives in such a way as to make one of the options more rational to everyone than the other options. In our case of the financing of public schools, if Pareto optimality does not in fact obtain when the choice is between levy proposal #1 and tax proposal #2, it may well exist when the choice is between, say, levy proposal #17 and tax proposal #23. This is to say, while Pareto optimality may not exist in the case of a particular set of options, it might seem plausible that one could be found.

Unfortunately, this revision approach to finding a distributively rational policy choice requires that two factual conditions obtain: (1) that someone actually find such a set of alternatives and (2) that each individual limit his calculations of the benefit/cost ratios to that set of alternatives that contains the Pareto-optimal choice (e.g., levy #17 and tax #23). Let us assume that policy proposers are sufficiently inventive to identify in fact a policy choice that would be Pareto-optimal (even though such an assumption requires that fate cooperate), so that we might attend to the second condition. If a person had been presented with, say, 25 variations on the levy alternative and as many tax

[21] For an example of the readjustment approach to distributive rationality, see Knut Wicksell, "A New Principle of Just Taxation," translated and reprinted in *Classics in the Theory of Public Finance,* ed. Richard A. Musgrave and Alan T. Peacock (London: Macmillan, 1958), pp. 72–118.

alternatives, though he may find levy #17 to be more advantageous than tax #23, if he were rational he would not limit his calculations to those two alternatives, but would, instead, insist on that levy or tax policy which has the highest benefit/cost ratio for him.[22] The revision approach to finding a distributively rational policy choice would, then, in fact work only if one could systematically induce amnesia in all members of the relevant public. So, then, the revision approach to finding a Pareto-optimal policy choice appears not too helpful as a procedure for actually coming up with such a choice.

A second way to cope with the remote likelihood that policy makers could hit upon a Pareto-optimal alternative would be to apply some sort of compensation principle in such a way as to convert some non-Pareto-optimal choice into a Pareto-optimal choice.[23] For illustration, let us take one of the patterns of preference from the case of the school financing policy that was not Pareto-optimal:

	Person A	**Person B**	**Person C**
(2)	levy	levy	tax

Recall that such a pattern says that persons A and B each believe that the benefit/cost ratio is higher for them, respectively, if they opt for the local levy rather than for the state income tax, and person C believes the contrary to be

[22] James S. Coleman makes the same criticism of the readjustment approach in "Beyond Pareto Optimality," in *Philosophy, Science and Method: Essays in Honor of Ernest Nagel*, ed. Sidney Morgenbesser, Patrick Suppes, and Morton White (New York: St. Martin's Press, 1969), p. 419.

[23] As Kenneth J. Arrow points out in *Social Choice and Individual Values* (2nd ed.; New York: John Wiley & Sons, 1963), p. 38, this is not the same compensation principle as that introduced into economic theory by Kaldor. The now classic Kaldor compensation principle does not even require that the compensation actually be paid.

true for him. If, in this case, person C could be compensated for the relative loss that he stands to suffer if the levy system is selected over the income tax, so that he too would stand to gain more if the levy policy were chosen, then the levy would be a distributively rational choice even though person C did not prefer it. That is, the actual compensating for person C's loss transforms a non-Pareto-optimal choice into a Pareto-optimal choice.

But the problems inherent in attaching a compensation principle to the notion of Pareto-optimal choice are especially knotty. If what constitutes compensation is left to the policy maker to decide, the procedure assumes that the policy maker has access to the subjective view of the "loser" and so could determine what would constitute adequate compensation. If, on the other hand, the decision as to what constitutes compensation is left to the loser himself, then for him to choose rationally he would have to demand *more* than "compensation." That is, to be rational, he would have to insist on the highest amount he thinks he could get. This being so, it might well be rational to try to always be deemed the loser (i.e., to declare that one prefers an option one does not in fact prefer, where one prefers the consequences of posing as the loser because of the anticipated "compensation"), for as such one might well stand to benefit more than if one were to be a winner.

Though the notion of a compensation principle does not seem to solve more problems than it creates, it does suggest a more sophisticated approach to a search for a description of distributive rationality that might in fact be useful for policy choices. Note that the way in which the compensation principle transforms a non-Pareto-optimal choice into a Pareto-optimal choice is that it allows at least one individual to view his policy choice as but one piece of a larger or complex choice, the point of which is to end up with the most favorable of perceived benefit/cost ratios.

Person C could *rationally* choose the levy option even though he preferred the tax option, for by opting for the levy policy and its attendant losses for him, he qualified himself for a gain (thanks to losers' compensation) that in the long run made the levy option more rational than the tax option. It is this notion of a complex choice that suggests a way to circumvent the difficulties in trying to achieve, on any single and simple choice, Pareto-optimal rationality. That is, if some policy choice can be rational to all members of the relevant public even *with* some members standing to lose directly from that policy, then a distributively rational policy choice need not entail Pareto-optimal rationality. In other words, there are other routes to rational consensus than through the Pareto optimal.

If it is the case that any collective (persons who constitute a relevant public) does over time make more than one choice, then it would seem rational for the individuals in that collective to calculate benefit/cost ratios not on a single simple-choice basis, but over the longer run. The reason that the longer-run view would be more rational is that not every choice is equally important to every individual. It is rational for an individual to barter in such a way as to "save up credits" by "giving in" on decisions that are less important to him, in order to gain more power or control in those decisions that are more important to him. The perception of choice as complex, combined with some sort of system, formal or informal, of political credit, allows for rational consensus in cases in which each person does not stand to directly gain by the choice. The response that this view of collective rationality suggests to the question of whether distributively rational policy choices are in fact possible is this: yes, if political exchanges are in fact possible. It would, then, seem that the more comprehensive and trusted the system of political crediting, the more likely it is that distributively rational policy choices can in fact be made.[24] Short of such a system, distributive rationality (as the strong sense of 'rational in the view of the relevant public') would not appear to be achievable consistently. Such being the case, decision procedures that can be used to cope with conflict of interest seem necessary to the making of policy choices that are at least in some sense collectively rational. The criteria for such decision procedures cannot themselves be justified by appeal to rationality, but must instead be decided by appeal to principles regarding what is right. It is to this and other normative issues embedded in the making of educational policy that we turn in chapter 4.

SUMMARY

After having reviewed the common senses in which choices might be thought rational, it was noted that for a policy choice to be rational in the strong sense: (1) the agent's reasons for the choice must make reference to a complete description of his policy goal; (2) the agent must take into account all facts that he believes to be relevant to the achievement of his goals; (3) the agent must use a decision method that he believes will contribute to the selection of a policy that, in turn, will contribute to the achievement of his policy goal; and (4) the agent must base his beliefs (2 and 3) on the findings of scientific inquiry. But to hold out for rationality in the strongest sense, it was further noted, would not under just any conditions be rational. In order to identify the sort of conditions under which policy is made, we distinguished five types of knowledge conditions (game conditions: certainty, risk, uncertainty; nongame conditions: partial ignorance, complete ignorance). Since most commonly policy choices are choices

---

[24] For a fuller development of this same general view, see Coleman, "Beyond Pareto Optimality."

under partial ignorance—knowledge conditions which thwart attempts at ideally rational choice—we abandoned our search for ideally rational policy choice in favor of models for less-than-ideally-rational, yet as-rational-as-possible policy choice.

Of these models for rational policy choice, the maximizing model proved untenable because it makes rational policy choice not in fact possible. The satisficing model was discarded, for it allows irrational choices. As a way to avoid these difficulties, a third model, contextual optimizing, was introduced—a model according to which a policy choice is rational if its benefit/cost ratio, in the view of the relevant public, is higher than that of any other perceived alternative. Since a necessary feature of the model is that the choice be rational *in the view of the relevant public,* we turned to a consideration of what might constitute such a case of collective rationality. Having distinguished two senses of collective rationality (distributive and preferential), we settled on a discussion of the stronger sense, distributive rationality. The problem lay not in describing a strong sense of collective rationality, but in describing it in a way that would make collectively rational policy choices in fact possible rather than just logical possibilities: finding directly a Pareto-optimal choice appears unlikely; revision of alternatives so as to create a Pareto-optimal choice would work only if it were possible systematically to induce amnesia; and using the compensation principle to arrive at a Pareto optimal could make deception the most rational choice. If, though, one allows the introduction of the notions of complex choices and political credits, and if such a system of political exchange is in fact possible, then collective rationality in the strong sense is in fact possible.

FOUR

THE JUSTIFICATION
OF
EDUCATIONAL POLICIES

ONE PREVALENT POPULAR VIEW of the activity of justifying educational policies is that it is a futile enterprise promoted by the politically naïve. Under this view, the politically savvy policy makers, having "a feel" for what policies will be accepted, propose only those policies that can in fact gain general acceptance. The first assumption of this view is that the members of the relevant public "know" what they want. That is, they already have opinions as to whether the benefit/cost ratios for particular policy proposals are favorable. The second and third assumptions are that the members of the public develop such opinions "automatically" and that such opinions are not readily influenced. Since the public's opinions of any category and level of policy are "ready-made givens," the appropriate role of the policy maker is that of a politician who is adroit in the conduct of "partisan mutual adjustment" until such time as a level of consensus that is sufficient for action is reached.[1] In this view, those who would concern themselves with such "philosophical" questions as whether a particular educational policy is justifiable are, at best, "out of touch with the real world." For example, if there is general consensus that schools should (or should not) be integrated by busing, that advertising should (or should not) be classified as "educationally potent" and therefore be required to meet specified educational criteria, or that children should (or should not) be compelled to attend school, then whether the particular policy is "justifiable" is irrelevant.[2]

A second popular view of the justification of educational policies is that it is a prudent step in policy making and that what it really boils down to is public relations work, or salesmanship. That is, the justification of a policy choice consists in the policy-maker's "communicating" to the public those rationales that the public will "buy." To justify a curricular policy for vocational education, for example, the policy maker qua sales agent must persuade or convince the public that it wants the "product." Typically, the sales pitch consists of an instrumental argument designed to persuade the "customer" that the policy will bring him something he wants, e.g., more job opportunities, fewer unskilled "freeloaders" on the welfare rolls, or earlier economic independence of children. One assumption of justification as selling is that the pitch that "works"—i.e., gains acceptance

[1] For discussion of partisan mutual adjustment, see Charles E. Lindblom, *The Intelligence of Democracy* (New York: Free Press, 1965), chaps. 3, 4, and 5; and idem, *The Policy-Making Process* (Englewood Cliffs, N.J.: Prentice-Hall, 1968), chap. 11.

[2] Under this "politician's view" of justification, results of an opinion poll can constitute sufficient "justification" to adopt, revise, or scrap any policy.

—is the right one. A second assumption is that the public can be brought to view a particular policy as basically beneficial, i.e., that anyone can be sold just about any policy, depending upon the "psychological strength" of the proffered rationale. Third, whether a policy ought to be allowed to "go" or not depends upon the results of the PR campaign. In brief, under this view, sound justification consists in sound advertising; "philosophical" considerations regarding justification come to bear only in those cases in which they are required for successful selling.

Under the politicking and selling views of justification, if the members of the public view a policy as advantageous or rational, then the policy is justifiable, no matter what the grounds for the respective judgments that the policy choice is rational. And if we were to require only that educational policy decisions be perceived as rational, then either of these views of justification would surely be adequate. But if we insist that educational policies be perceived as rational on the *right* grounds or for *good* reasons, then we must look beyond politicking and selling for a stronger sense of justification. Further, if we prize effective and moral policy choices, then we must insist that the politicking and selling accounts of justification are inadequate. Only a modicum of imagination or historical knowledge is required to recognize that policies "justified" by political bartering or successful advertising can be and too often have been doomed to ineffectiveness (e.g., numerous "innovative" policies in education) or have been morally or aesthetically atrocious (e.g., Nazi anti-Semitic educational policies and the rigid restrictions of revolutionary art to standards of "socialist realism"), or both. Another way to see the inadequacies of bartering and advertising as modes of justification of any social policy, including educational policies, is this. To bring the public around to wanting a particular policy does not entail that the public *should* want the policy. That is, one can want or prefer a policy, or believe a policy to be beneficial, for the wrong reasons—reasons that do not satisfy objective or non-arbitrary criteria for rationality both as a scientific and normative concept.

The response from the politician and the PR agent might be "Yes, but . . .": Yes, people sometimes express preferences for policies that they should not want, but the political system functions on political bartering, not on a popular demand that policies should be made for the "philosophically right" reasons. Or, yes, with smoothly run sales campaigns one can sell even garbage, but without such campaigns few social policies could be implemented without resistance. I suspect that insofar as the general public fails to reflect critically and carefully on social policy choices and in the extent to which people have yet to learn to demand *good* reasons, the politician's "partisan mutual adjusting" and the PR agent's sales pitch will continue to be useful to social action. But to concede that point is not to agree that justification should be reduced to political bartering and advertising, lest the very concept of justification be lost, along with our criteria for good judgment.[3] Moreover, it should perhaps be noted that, at least at present, the number of persons who are willing to accept or "buy" a particular policy does not add or detract from the soundness of the reasons in support of the policy. Only if we could develop *very* successful educational policies would acceptance or "purchase" imply soundness of reasons, and then only contingently so. The question for this chapter, then, is *not*, what are the conditions under which people will accept policy decisions? Rather, it is, *what must be true to say that we should accept a policy choice?* In other words, what are

[3] For a discussion of 'good judgment,' see Thomas F. Green, *The Activities of Teaching* (New York: McGraw-Hill, 1971), chap. 8.

the objective or nonarbitrary tests that a policy must pass before we should adopt it or judge it favorably? An answer to that question undergirds sound policy making and criticism. Yet, we should note, it is that question to which the models for rational policy choice (maximizing, satisficing, and contextual optimizing as discussed in chapter 3) are indifferent, as they require only that each person "have an opinion" and so are neutral with regard to the grounds for those opinions.

Let us look more closely at the question: what must be true to say that we should accept a policy choice? Two points might be helpful. First, it is important to be clear at the outset about what the question does *not* ask. It does not call for a listing of features that are specific to any particular policy. Rather, it demands the logical conditions that would have to be met for us to judge any policy to be acceptable qua justifiable on good grounds. Recall that in chapter 1 we queried what must be true of a plan for action to say that it is a policy. In response we produced four general, logical conditions that any plan for action whatsoever must meet if it is to count as a policy:

1. Some authorizing agent (A_a) obligates itself to direct some implementing agent (A_i) to act in accord with a specified conditional imperative (I);

2. The conditional imperative (I) must be of the form, Do something which satisfies the conditions for some specified X-ing whenever, without exception, specified conditions C occur;

3. The authorizing agent (A_a) undertakes the obligation (condition 1) for the purpose of effecting some specified state of affairs (S) and to do so without violating any restrictive rules (R) by which A_a would claim to abide;

> 4. The authorizing agent's obligation can be re-
> vised and yet not be violated *both* if the authoriz-
> ing agent announces his revision of the conditional
> imperative from *I* to *I'* to those persons who can
> bring about conditions *C* and *C' and* if the autho-
> rizing agent gives consideration due the views of
> the relevant public as defined by the political and
> moral contexts of the initial policy decision and its
> revision.

In a similar fashion, we here seek a set of conditions that must obtain if any policy is to qualify as one that can (logically) be supported on good grounds.

Second, the question, what must be true to say that we should accept a policy choice?, is not one that arises only in "academic" exercises. The reason, I suspect, that it might appear somewhat exotic and "removed" is this. Most often, when as policy maker or critic we face the question, it is directed to a particular policy rather than policies in general. For example, legislators might ask themselves whether a particular finance policy proposal (bill) for schooling merits their votes. (Recall that this is to be kept distinct from the question of whether supporting the bill would be "politically" advantageous.) Or, a school administrator might ask of an existing evaluation-of-teaching policy, what could be done to improve this policy? Or, one might undertake to review some existing policy to determine whether it ought to be revised. Whether we are faced with the task of judging a policy before or after it has been implemented, for the purpose of deciding whether it ought or ought not to be revised in some way, we must first know how to judge the policy in question. That is, we must know what evaluative tests the policy would have to pass in order to qualify as justifiable or normatively rational. In each of these cases, we are in essence asking what must be true of this policy (or any other policy) for us to say that we should approve of it, though we typically formulate our particular question in somewhat different terms.

THE DESIRABILITY TEST

With any activity for which there are developed skills, techniques, tools, and the like, one can attempt to bring about various states of affairs by engaging in that activity. In farming a thousand acres, for example, one can try to grow a thousand acres of artichokes, a thousand acres of blueberries, a thousand acres of wheat, or a thousand acres of any other vegetable, fruit, or grain, or any combination thereof. Or, one could aim at growing a thousand acres of weeds. Further, in the context of any such developed activity, one can design policies to serve as vehicles for achieving such state-of-affairs purposes (S-purposes). The developed activities in which are located the curricular, methodological, resource-allocation, and distributional policies that, as established in chapter 2, are necessary to the conduct of education are numerous and varied. They include, but are not limited to teaching; law-making on all levels; administering of institutions, institutional agencies, and programs ranging from HEW and the U.S. Office of Education to the social science department of Mountainview Middle School and from the FCC to the media room at the local library; and "parenting." Much as in farming one can choose policies the point of which is to grow a thousand acres of weeds, so in making educational policies of any category one can settle on policies the point of which is less than desirable. That is, while having a policy logically entails that the agent undertake the obligation (condition 1) for the purpose of effecting some state of affairs S, it does not entail that S be desirable. Or, perhaps more directly put, just because one has a policy does not mean that he should want to achieve the state of affairs for which the policy was designed.

When we face the issue so directly it seems even painfully obvious that no matter how cleverly conceived and ingeniously designed a policy might be, if its S-purposes are not commendable, then the policy is not a good one. Further, it would seem that persons who are in a position to make or remake educational policies generally wish to make and support only justifiable policies. Yet, not uncommonly, established policies are continued simply because they are there or because they are "traditional," [4] without so much as a question to determine what the policies' purposes are, much less whether those states of affairs are desirable. Also, all too frequently, new policies are adopted without reference to the purposes they are to serve. Preoccupied with the power of a hammer or the interesting marks that can be made with a crayon, small children have been known to apply the hammer or crayon indiscriminately, without a thought to the desirability of the state of affairs thus achieved. Likewise, preoccupied with the most recent educational fads, educational policy makers have been known to adopt policies to promote those fads without a careful consideration of the desirability of the resulting state of affairs. In the indiscriminate adoption of policies to promote the individualization of instruction, career education, child-centeredness, nongradedness, open-concept education, performance-based training, and many others, too commonly the question of what states of affairs are sought is never broached. Thus the evaluation question, are the states of

[4] For a clear, brief critical analysis of the argument that we ought to continue or adopt particular practices or policies "because they are traditional," see Harold Weisberg, "Tradition and the Traditionalist," in *Philosophy and Education*, ed. Israel Scheffler (2nd ed.; Boston: Allyn & Bacon, 1966), pp. 349–57.

affairs at which the policies are aimed desirable? can hardly arise.

At this point it should be clear that for a policy to be justifiable or normatively rational it must be desirable, but without further qualifications such a formulation of the condition may allow too much. Consider again the farmer who decides on a policy of trying to grow a thousand acres of weeds each year. The policy appears to be a poor one because the S-purpose seems undesirable. But it should be noted that the S-purpose seems undesirable because we view the policy as a food-production policy. If the farmer intended his policy as a food-production policy, then we are doubtlessly right in assessing it a poor policy: weeds do not count as food. But suppose that our farmer is working on the development of a new, safer means for weed control and needs a thousand acres of weeds for experimentation. Judged as an experimental resource policy, it would appear to be desirable insofar as its purpose is desirable. In both cases the S-purpose of the policy is the same, namely, to grow a thousand acres of weeds. What differs is the basis of our evaluation, i.e., the set of criteria we use to determine whether the S-purpose passes muster. Only to say, then, that an educational policy's S-purpose must be desirable for the policy to be justifiable may not be enough. We might want to add that the S-purpose must be desirable as an educational policy.

This point is no nice subtlety or subtle nicety for the development of mental adroitness. Many are the times in which educational policies have been implemented or scrapped because their purposes were judged on an inappropriate set of criteria. The reduction of a curriculum to a small number of "basic" courses may be commendable curricular policy if assessed on money-saving criteria, but not if judged on educational criteria. A standard, fixed curriculum for all students might be desirable as a policy's

S-purpose if one interprets it as a management purpose, but not if one takes it to be an educational purpose.[5] Taxing policies designed to bolster the budget of educational television may have desirable S-purposes if viewed as educational policies, but undesirable purposes if viewed as "vote-getting" policies. The point is, for a curricular, methodological, resource-allocation, or distributional policy to be *educationally* justifiable, its S-purpose must be justifiable as an *educational* purpose.

Here we should consider what constitutes an *educational* purpose, for until we have an answer to that question we shall not be able to determine when a policy's purpose is justifiable as an educational purpose. This question should not be confused with that of chapter 2, what are educational *policies*? Our response to that question was that educational policies consist of those categories of policies (curricular, methodological, resource-allocation, and distributional) that are necessary to the systematic conduct of education. The point here is to distinguish between judging the *purposes* of policies of these categories on *educational* criteria and assessing those purposes on *noneducational* grounds. It may seem puzzling at first to say that one can make educational policies that do not have educational purposes. That puzzlement disappears on recalling from chapter 2 that just some content, method, resources, and distribution are necessary to the conduct of education. "Some" content, etc., *can* be specified in policies of which the purposes are economic, managerial, or directed toward any other noneducational consideration. If we wish to assess educational policy on educational grounds, however, then we shall have to judge desirable only those educational

---

[5] For an astonishing plethora of examples of such elevation of management purposes over educational purposes in American education, see Raymond Callahan, *Education and the Cult of Efficiency* (Chicago: University of Chicago Press, 1962).

policies that have educational purposes. This is *not* to say that educational policies should never be judged on noneducational (e.g., economic) criteria. Perhaps most should be judged on noneducational grounds as well, so as to improve the health and longevity of educational enterprises in the multiplicity of contexts in which education must be conducted. The point, instead, is this: (1) to say that an educational policy is desirable when assessed on *some* criteria should not be misunderstood to mean that it necessarily serves educational purposes; and (2) if an educational policy serves no educational purpose, then it logically cannot be judged to be justifiable on educational grounds, i.e., if an educational policy is justifiable only on noneducational grounds, then it is not justifiable on educational grounds.

Having clarified what is at issue, let us return to the question: what constitutes an *educational* purpose? If, as in chapter 2, we take the general purpose of education to be the development of at least some beliefs, attitudes, skills, dispositions, values, or tastes, then we can say that such would have to be true of any purpose in order for it to be educational in any sense. That is, to determine that a purpose is educational under any interpretation, it must make reference to the development of at least some belief, attitude, etc. But for a purpose to be educational under a particular description, that purpose must make reference specifically to some belief, attitude, etc., that the particular view of education prescribes. If, as some suggest, the purposes of education are derivative of one's view of an ideal society, way of life, or some such,[6] then the fuller form of response would be that a purpose is desirable as an educational purpose when it refers to the development of at least

[6] For one especially clear development of the view that the purposes of education are derivative, see T. F. Daveney, "Education— A Moral Concept," in *New Essays in the Philosophy of Education,* ed. Glenn Langford and D. J. O'Connor (London: Routledge & Kegan Paul, 1973), pp. 79–95.

some belief, attitude, etc., that in turn is justifiable by appeal to principles that define one's view of an ideal way of life or the like. In other words, an *educational* purpose is one that promotes or is constitutive of a person's developing beliefs, attitudes, etc., in whatever direction or directions are deemed conducive to or constitutive of the Good Life under some description.

To demonstrate one use of the distinction between educational and noneducational purposes of educational policies, I present here a principle based on that distinction. Though this principle can be defended, I do not attempt a defense here, but offer it as illustrative material only. That principle is as follows: In order to be justifiable, an educational policy must have at least some educational purpose. That is, an educational policy that has no *educational* purpose is not desirable.

I draw an example of an application of this principle from Soviet sociological literature.[7] Given that some factory jobs are uninteresting to persons who have completed secondary school, Soviet industrial management faces the problem of a high rate of turnover of workers and the concomitant loss of productivity. Sociologists conceived of two ways to solve the problem. One proposed solution consisted in denying some persons the opportunity to reach such a high level of education in order that the factory jobs would appear interesting to them and productivity would increase. The other proposal was to alter the jobs in such a way as to increase their content rather than to alter the distributional policy of education for noneducational purposes. Because the all-round development of the individual (an edu-

[7] I take this example from A. G. Zdravomyslov, V. P. Rozhin, and V. A. Yadov, eds., *Chelovek i ego rabota* [Man and His Work] (Moscow: Izdatel'stvo "Mysl'," 1967), pp. 283–85. I do not know whether the solution that these sociologists suggested was actually adopted.

cational purpose) is valued over economic productivity and, for that matter, over all other noneducational purposes, the first solution was rejected since it would have *replaced* the educational purpose of an educational policy with a noneducational purpose.

To recap, three alternative tests regarding the desirability of a policy's S-purposes might be put to any educational policy to determine whether that policy is justifiable in the sense of being normatively rational. If the policy should fail the one of these tests that is deemed appropriate, then it is not justifiable. The *first* test is not peculiar to educational policies, but is a general test that asks only whether the policy's S-purpose is, under *some* interpretation, desirable. With this test, *no* distinction is made between differing contents of criteria, so that a policy is given a failing mark on this test only if no set of criteria, whatever its content, can be found which the policy's S-purpose satisfies. The *second* test would have us determine whether the educational policy is educationally justifiable, that is, whether the policy has some *educational* purpose. An educational policy that fails this test could still be judged justifiable if its purpose were desirable when assessed on the grounds of some noneducational criteria. This test differs from the first in that it distinguishes educational from noneducational purposes. The *third* and strongest test, which is identified but not defended in this section, requires that any educational policy's S-purpose be defensible on educational grounds. More specifically, to pass the third test, the educational policy's S-purpose must *at least* promote or be constitutive of some person or persons' developing beliefs, attitudes, etc., in whatever way or ways are deemed conducive to or constitutive of the Good Life under some description. If, then, the third test is applied, a policy's S-purpose might meet noneducational criteria and yet fail to be justifiable.

THE EFFECTIVENESS TEST

Let us imagine some educational policy, the purpose of which passes the strongest S-purpose test, in that its S-purpose is defensible on educational grounds. For illustration, let us say that the S-purpose which constitutes the goal of the policy is that state of affairs in which all persons in the society appreciate the sounds of the didgeridoo. If, further, we allow the appreciation of sounds of the didgeridoo as part and parcel of the Good Life, then this educational policy is justifiable on educational grounds. The rest of the policy may be described thus: The Minister of Mass Communication has directed all radio and television station managers to play or have played recordings of the didgeridoo for the first three minutes of each day's transmission. That is, the station managers (A_i) are to play three minutes of didgeridoo sounds (X), whenever the station is just beginning its transmission for the day (C). Now, even if we assume that the Minister of Mass Communication has both de jure and de facto authority to direct the managers to play didgeridoo recordings or, still stronger, that the managers do in fact do as directed, it is still quite unlikely that we would judge this particular educational policy to be worthy of support. Though its purpose may be indisputably educational, the proposed means (A_i's X-ing whenever C obtains) appears ineffective as a tool for promoting the appreciation of didgeridoo sounds. So it would seem that while educational S-purposes may be necessary to justifiable educational policies, such appears not to be sufficient. Rather, to be justifiable a policy must also specify means that would appear likely to effect the specified S-purposes.

It is with an interest in placing the effectiveness test in bold relief that I have selected such an outlandish example. And I am aware that the point may appear so obvious as not even to need any exemplification, much less the overdrawn example I have provided. Yet, it is a point that not uncommonly is missed. In educational policy circles it is fairly ordinary to witness a dispute over some policy proposal which in form goes as follows:

> **Policy Advocate:** If we adopt a policy of requiring teachers to attend sensitivity-training sessions, then our students will develop positive self-concepts.
>
> **Policy Critic:** I've seen what those sensitivity sessions are like. Anyone who thinks that those sessions can do anything constructive is really misguided.
>
> **Advocate:** But you don't understand; without a positive self-concept, a person's educational development is stymied.
>
> **Critic:** But *you* don't understand; sensitivity training is a hoax.

However fuzzily stated the policy's purpose and however flimsy the empirical claim and weak the challenge, the point to be made is this. In our advocate's view, if a policy's purpose is a good one, then the policy is good. Period. Any challenge to the policy he would interpret as a challenge to the policy's purpose and so recommence a defense of the purpose. Our critic, preoccupied with what he perceives as an ineffective means for achieving any purposes, is able to focus only on the empirical claim. Such a critic, so preoccupied, too frequently judges a policy as justifiable if it has an effective means, without regard to the desirability of the purpose. So if it is to the reader disconcertingly obvious that the means (i.e., A's X-ing whenever C obtains) must be likely to effect S for the policy to be justifiable, perhaps my examples could serve to point out how arguments based on this misunderstanding go wrong.

Once again, I should like to acknowledge that it does

seem obvious that if the means of the policy under scrutiny is not effective as a tool for achieving that policy's purposes, then the policy would not be justifiable. As noted in policy condition 3, the very point of the agent's undertaking the policy obligation (condition 1) is to effect some specified state of affairs S. So a policy that seems to have little or no chance of achieving its purposes would not seem supportable. To be sure, an impressive body of literature (under the rubric "evaluation research"[8]) has been developed especially over the last ten years or so in response to the question of how can we figure out whether a particular policy or program of policies is achieving its goal (here, S-purposes). In that literature, the problems inherent in deciding whether the means is effective are essentially the basic problems of social science research in general. The claim 'A's X-ing whenever C is likely to effect S' is an empirical claim which is as testable as any other empirical claim. Problems in testing the claim are viewed as matters of "controlling and correcting." And if one has used the strongest feasible empirical test, given the restrictions of the particular "action setting," then one has determined, insofar as is possible, whether "A's X-ing whenever C obtains" is likely to effect S. Unlike the test for educational purposes, the test for effectiveness rests not on an appeal to the Good Life, but on an appeal to the results of empirical research.

Now we come to the part that is perhaps not so obvious. Given the results of an empirical test of an effectiveness claim, exactly what is to be made of those results is not so clear. Let us say that a policy of individualized mathematics instruction has been implemented for purposes of increas-

---

[8] For an excellent survey of the problems of evaluation research and an extensive bibliography that includes many items of particular interest to educators, see Carol H. Weiss, *Evaluation Research* (Englewood Cliffs, N.J.: Prentice-Hall, 1972).

ing the rate of achievement as measured by specified standardized tests. Let us also say that the effectiveness test applied six weeks after the policy's implementation shows no increase in the rate of achievement. Should that be taken to mean that the policy fails the effectiveness test and so is not justifiable? Or should the test be run again at twelve weeks or twenty-four weeks into the period in which the policy has been in effect? Or when? The point here is that to say that a policy must pass an effectiveness test in order to be justifiable is correct, but not always helpful. Or, if we take a case in which we wish to determine prior to a proposed policy's implementation whether it should be implemented, the question becomes: is A's X-ing whenever C obtains likely to effect S? In this case the test of the empirical claim will be done by looking at studies of similar monitored policies that have already been evaluated or a pilot study or some such. Here one wonders how strong the supportable claim would have to be for the policy to be justifiable. Must "A's X-ing whenever C obtains" be "very likely" to effect S? Or will "quite likely" suffice? If the S-purpose is desirable enough (e.g., a cure for cancer) then perhaps even "remotely likely" would be enough for the policy to pass the effectiveness test.

In general we would, I suspect, say that whatever means which, ceteris paribus, is the most likely of perceived means to effect S passes the effectiveness test, even if the means is only remotely likely to effect S.[9] In other words, the fact that no means is *certain* to effect S and the fact that some means are more likely than others to effect S together suggest that whatever else might be true of the effectiveness test, it must be a relative one. Since innumerable means

[9] The qualifier 'ceteris paribus' is necessary here, for, as we shall see, restrictive purposes supersede or override S-purposes. What is needed here is that means which both does not violate any restrictive purposes and is the most likely to effect the S-purpose, in that order.

might be effective to some degree, the point would be to select the most effective of the perceived lot. If the schema is reminiscent of contextual optimizing (see chapter 3), it should be no surprise, for when one is choosing rationally under that description he is choosing the best of perceived alternatives.

The question now becomes, is the effectiveness test reducible to the problem of rational choice? If policies could have only once-achievable and repeatedly achievable S-purposes, to select the most effective means would be to make the most rational choice. But policies can have another type of S-purpose which, as discussed in chapter 1, is logically unachievable. Given that status of unachievability of some policies' S-purposes, it is not clear what is to be understood by "A's X-ing whenever C obtains is likely to effect S." That is, to ask whether something is likely to effect a state of affairs that logically cannot be effected makes little sense. As before, the solution appears to formulate the test as a relative one: a policy employing that means which is likely to effect a state of affairs that is more similar to S than any other state of affairs that any other perceived means might effect is the most effective policy.

But an additional problem arises when dealing with unachievable policies. Should we judge more effective that policy means which is *very likely to effect* Q or that means which is only *somewhat likely to effect* R, where R resembles the unachievable, ideal X more closely than does Q? This problem shares the general features of the decision under uncertainty discussd in chapter 3. Much as in the case of the decision of whether to select the metal ball from the left or right urn, which policy ought to be judged more effective in such a predicament depends upon whether the judge is an optimist or a pessimist. The optimist, or risk taker, would judge the "somewhat likely" means to be more effective than the "very likely" means, for it at least gives him a chance at that state of affairs R which more closely resembles S. The pessimist, or cautious judge, would have to deem the "very likely" means to be the more effective, for it is more likely to deliver at least some goods, here Q.

Especially since a good many of our educational policy S-purposes are unachievable, the evaluation literature can be misleading, for it focuses on *achievable* S-purposes only. For example, a widely used distinction between formative evaluation and summative evaluation is generally employed in such a way as to suggest that any policy (even those with unachievable S-purposes) can be evaluated in either way.[10] Whether formative or summative evaluation is appropriate depends on whether the point of the evaluation, respectively, is to provide information that might be helpful in the improvement of the policy in question or to determine whether the policy ought to be abandoned in favor of another. That is, formative evaluation provides "feedback on the basis of which [one can] produce *revisions*," [11] while summative evaluation consists in a review for purposes of not revising the policy but deciding whether the policy ought either to be adopted more widely or abandoned altogether. The formative/summative evaluation distinction can be useful when identifying the role that evaluation of policies with unachievable purposes can play, but as the distinction is commonly used it can be seriously misleading.

An example of a methodological policy of teaching illustrates my point. Imagine that a teacher of ballet has the unachievable S-purpose of getting her students to do the

[10] Michael Scriven introduced this distinction in "The Methodology of Evaluation," in *Perspectives of Curriculum Evaluation,* American Educational Research Association Monograph No. 1 on Curriculum Evaluation, ed. Ralph W. Tyler, Robert M. Gagné, and Michael Scriven (Chicago: Rand McNally, 1967), pp. 39–83.
[11] Ibid., p. 43. Emphasis added.

basic steps perfectly. Over years of teaching, she has discovered that she obtains the best results when she video-
tapes each student individually for a playback session in
which each student criticizes herself in the presence of the
instructor. Here "best results" does not mean the S-purpose
is actually achieved. It means, rather, that such results
resemble the S-purpose more closely than the results of any
other teaching method employed to that point.

Notice that if someone who employs the formative/
summative distinction, as it is commonly used, were responsible for the terminal evaluation of our ballet teacher's
methodological policy, no matter how effective the teacher's
policy, the evaluator would give it failing marks. Let us say
that the teacher spends the first six months of instruction
on the basic steps, at which point the evaluator appears to
assess the policy's effectiveness. After being told what would
constitute a perfect performance of the basic steps, the
evaluator watches the novices perform. Because the evaluator believes it appropriate to use summative evaluation
at the end of instruction units, the evaluator assesses the
policy by comparing the results with the S-purpose. No
matter how fine the performances, the evaluator would always have to say that the S-purpose had not been achieved.
And he would be right, but his observation would be irrelevant. If one were to apply summative evaluation to policies
with unachievable S-purposes, one would always give the
policy failing marks, no matter how effective it is.[12]

To avoid such a travesty on the concept of evaluation,
it is necessary to recognize that policies with unachievable
purposes are amenable only to formative evaluation, and
then only in a special comparative form. That is, if a teacher

---

[12] The reader who is familiar with the Scriven paper will
recognize that my example assumes "payoff" procedures in both the
formative and summative roles for evaluation. See ibid., pp. 53–55.

tries only one methodological policy and gets result R, when the S-purpose is unachievable, the evaluator could only judge whether R resembles S more or less than the present state of affairs P. If the teacher tries policy q and its revised version r and gets result Q and R respectively, the evaluator can then assess whether Q or R (or the present state of affairs P) resembles S more closely. Viewed from a slightly different angle, the point is this: if the purpose of making some policy is to approach a state of affairs as closely as possible rather than to achieve it, to evaluate any such policy one must *compare q* and *r* policy results with the unachievable goal *for the purpose* of measuring "distances" between results and the unachievable S rather than to see whether the S-purpose has actually been achieved. The point, then, of the evaluation of policies with unachievable purposes can logically be only to determine whether the policy is "on track" and approaching the S-purpose and whether the revision is "on track." Such is the point of formative evaluation.

THE JUSTNESS TEST

To this point we have established that if a policy is to be justifiable, the policy must pass at least two tests: (1) the S-purpose must be desirable and (2) "A's X-ing whenever C obtains" must be an effective means for achieving (or approaching) the S-purpose. To demonstrate that these tests alone are insufficient as tests for the justifiability of an educational policy, let us consider cases of policies that pass both tests on their strongest readings but yet would not count as justifiable. That is, let us examine policies that *both* have S-purposes that are justifiable as educational purposes *and* specify means that are very likely to achieve the S-purposes.

Let the first be a case of a distributional policy of education, the purpose of which is to ensure that some persons acquire mathematical and scientific knowledge of a level necessary to the continuous development of scientific knowledge. For this example, it must be imagined that the continuous development of scientific knowledge by at least some individuals is justifiable qua essential to some view of the Good Life. Let the means be specified as follows: The state superintendent of instruction (A_a) directs district school boards (A_i) to allocate annually 100 percent of the district's funds for mathematics and science instruction to the instruction of those students who are white and have parents who are college graduates whose annual income is at least $20,000 (to X whenever C obtains). It might be noted in passing that though this policy mentions the allocation of funds, it is a distributional rather than a resource policy. Rather than affect the resources dedicated to the conduct of mathematics and science education, it specifies to whom the particular educational content is to be directed. Let it further be the case that good evidence is available to support the claim that the specified means is very likely to effect the level of mathematical and scientific knowledge that constitutes the S-purpose.

Even if we grant that the S-purpose is desirable and that "A's X-ing whenever C" is an effective means for achieving S, the policy does not count as justifiable in that it is not *right* for "A to X whenever C obtains." Some might point out that it is not right in the sense that it is illegal. That is, it discriminates against nonwhite students or those whose parents are not college graduates and earn less than $20,000 per annum, either group of which might in this case be argued to be, in terms of constitutional law, a suspect class. Others might point out that the policy is not right apart from its legal status. They might instead argue that it is not right because it basis unequal treatment on irrelevant factors. Here the argument might be that demonstrated ability or achievement in mathematics and science would be an appropriate basis for discrimination, while skin color and the educational and financial status of parents are not appropriate bases for discrimination.

For a second example of a policy that passes both the desirability-of-S-purpose test and the effectiveness test, yet which fails to be justifiable, consider the case in which a principal makes a policy that denies parents of students access to the students' official records. That is, whenever parents request access to their children's official records, the principal shall deny the request. For purposes of illustration, let us further assume that the principal has in mind a defensible educational purpose and that his X-ing whenever C obtains is very likely to achieve that purpose. On being denied access to the records, a parent may object on the basis that the principal's policy contradicts district policy and therefore it is not right for him to X whenever C obtains. The district superintendent, on hearing of the principal's policy, may argue that the principal's X-ing whenever C obtains is not right because it contradicts a federal law. Though for different reasons, both the parent and the superintendent would be claiming that the policy is unjustifiable not because anything is wrong with its purpose (indeed they may even be unaware of its purpose) and not because its means is ineffective, but because the means is not *right*.

The central point here is that even though one may find the educational purposes of some policy to be desirable *and* believe on the basis of solid empirical evidence that the policy's means can in fact achieve those purposes, he may still have good reason to judge the policy unjustifiable on the grounds that the means (A's X-ing whenever C obtains) is not right. Further, as the two above cases of unjustifiable policies exemplify, to say that a policy is not right is to say any one of a number of things, all of which refer to the policy's means. To assert that a policy is not right may be to claim that it is legally wrong or morally wrong or that it contradicts some religious tenets which regard right action or some higher level (more "outer" in the nesting) policy or that it violates the rules of some game in which "A's X-ing whenever C obtains" counts as an action. In order, then, for policies to be right, whatever means are selected for achieving desirable purposes, those means must satisfy the restrictive principles (R-purposes) which define the "games" in the context of which the policy is made. Or, in terms of the policy conditions established in chapter 1, the point could roughly be put thus: for a policy to be justifiable, the agent must actually fulfill his obligation not to violate any restrictive rules R by which he would claim to abide. (Recall that policy condition 3 states that the authorizing agent [A_a] undertakes the obligation [condition 1] for the purpose of effecting some specified state of affairs [S] and to do so *without violating any restrictive rules* [R] *by which* A_a *would claim to abide.*)

But to be correct the point must be refined, for simply because some specified "A's X-ing whenever C obtains" does not violate those sets of rules with which the agent would claim to abide, the policy is not necessarily *right*. Hitler's directing persons to be killed whenever they were discovered to be Jews, for example, might not have violated any restrictive rules according to which Hitler would have claimed to abide, yet many would not hesitate to say that the policy was not right.

In a less hideous, though perhaps no less wrong policy case, a teacher may have a distribution policy according to which he discriminates between students on irrelevant or otherwise unsupportable grounds. That is, while a teacher's distribution policy may not violate the rules by which he claims to abide, those rules may themselves be unjust.

To make the example more specific, let us say that, given a consistently insufficient number of animal specimens for each student to have one to dissect, the biology teacher always allows only those students whose last names begin with *A* through *M* to participate in the lab section of the course. The teacher may claim that the policy is right because it does not violate his rule that when learning opportunities are in short supply, those students whose last names fall in the first half of the alphabet will be favored. In this case we would agree that the policy is subjectively right in the sense that it accords with his rule, but objectively wrong in the sense that the rule with which it accords is unjust.

In other words, a policy's jibing with some rule or rules is not a sufficient condition for its rightness in the sense of its being a justifiable policy. The third test for justifiability might, then, state that *the restrictive rules with which the means* ("A's X-*ing whenever* C *obtains*") *accords must be just.* Or, more directly, "A's X-*ing whenever* C *obtains*" *must be just.*

This is a stronger formulation of the third test than might at first appear. Notice that even though the policy in question might satisfy the restrictive purposes defined by the S-purposes of a more "outer" or higher level policy, but still not qualify as justifiable, those restrictive purposes might themselves be unjust. Moreover, the policy might accord with all relevant laws and yet not pass the third test of justifiability because the laws themselves might be unjust. The same point might correctly be made of any other R-purposes that the agent might bring to bear in his policy decision. Another way to put essentially the same point and at the same time to tie the point to some of the policy-relevant literature is this. Whether one thinks of rules that restrict the selection of means as constraining principles,[13] planning principles,[14] principles of procedure,[15] or some other such, it is principles of justice that take precedence in a determination of whether the policy passes the third test of justifiability, the just-means test.

Why, it might be asked, should principles of justice be taken to override other sorts of restrictive principles? [16] A proper response would require a considerable detour into the literature of moral philosophy and, more particularly, into considerations of justice as a moral concept. Very briefly, and I hope not too misleadingly, it might be said that the reason that principles of justice *override* any other restrictive principles is that principles of justice define how persons *ought* to stand in relationship to one another and so specify how conflicts of ideals or interests [17] *ought* to be handled. One might, on introducing someone to the game of chess, point to an official book of chess rules and say, "If you wish to play chess, you must play by these rules." Like-

[13] Carl G. Hempel, "Rational Action," *Proceedings and Addresses of the American Philosophical Association* 35 (1962): 7. Hempel's examples of constraining principles are "moral and legal norms, contractual commitments, social conventions, the rules of the game being played, or the like."

[14] Abraham Kaplan, "On the Strategy of Social Planning," *Policy Sciences* 4, no. 1 (March 1973): esp. 53.

[15] R. S. Peters, "Must an Educator Have an Aim?," in his *Authority, Responsibility and Education* (3rd ed.; London: George Allen & Unwin, 1973), p. 131.

[16] In the literature of moral philosophy this question takes the following form: how can we account for moral considerations' overriding or superseding other considerations?

[17] While for the most part discussion of justice in the literature of moral philosophy focuses on the conflict of *interests,* as R. M. Hare points out, it may be less misleading to talk of the conflict of interests that concerns moral philosophy as the conflict of not just any wants persons may have, but in particular wants that persons have when they believe whatever they want to be "means, necessary or sufficient, for the attainment of something which [they want] (or may want)." *Freedom and Reason* (London: Oxford University Press, 1963), p. 157.

wise, one might point to principles of justice and say, "If you want to make policies that are morally justifiable, then you shall have to adopt policies that accord with principles of justice, even if that means acting in disaccord with other restrictive principles which you might otherwise find applicable."

As illustration, let us say that a principal of a school wishes to make a distributional policy regarding which students are to have access to instruction in physical fitness. If the district policy on physical fitness instruction specifies that the program for boys should be assigned 80 percent of the instructional staff and equipment and the girls' program only 20 percent, then to act in accord with the more outer, district level policy, the principal would have to design his distributional policy, whatever his S-purposes in making the policy, in such a way that "A's X-ing whenever C obtains" would accord with the 80–20 percent principle. If, though, the 80–20 principle disaccords with a principle of justice which, for example, specifies that inequalities in treatment are unjust unless it is "reasonable to expect that they will work out to *everyone's* advantage," [18] short of a demonstration that everyone would benefit from the unequal treatment, a percentage principle that specifies any other than the percentages of boys and girls actually enrolled in the school would not be justifiable.

If we were to specify the principles of justice, we would be doing substantive or normative moral philosophy, an enterprise that outstrips the purpose of this essay. But whatever one specifies as principles of justice, it might be noted that the social function of such principles in general

[18] It is for purposes of illustration and *not* recommendation that I borrow this principle from John Rawls, "Justice as Fairness," *Philosophical Review* 67, no. 2 (April 1958): 165. Available also through the Bobbs-Merrill Reprint Series in Philosophy, Phil-174.

is to provide a *moral* way to decide between conflicting interests.[19] (Insofar, then, as a system of civil law specifies moral ways of adjudicating conflicting claims, it may correctly be said that it constitutes a system of justice.) Notice that while the question of desirability of S-purposes of a policy could arise outside the social context, the question of the justness of R-purposes could not. Further, if it were somehow impossible for anyone ever to act contrary to the interests of another person, the justness question could not arise, though we could still think of better states of affairs (S-purposes) toward which we might strive. And if we were unable to acknowledge principles as bearing impartially on our own conduct as well as the conduct of others, then again the just-means question would not arise, though one could still maintain visions of the Good Life. Because educational policy is typically made in social contexts, because it is not impossible for persons' interests to conflict, and because we are able to and do, as moral agents, acknowledge principles as applying impartially to both our own and others' conduct, for a policy to be justifiable the justness question must be answered affirmatively if the policy is to be considered justifiable in the fullest sense.

A fanatical utilitarian [20] might suggest that cases may occur in which we may not want to insist that the policy means be just in order for the policy to be judged justifiable. Consider, the fanatic utilitarian would suggest, a case of a *very* desirable S-purpose which we could achieve only by

---

[19] From Aristotle on, questions of what is moral have taken two distinct forms: (1) what is good or to what should men's actions aim? and (2) how should persons stand in relation to one another? (See *Nicomachean Ethics,* books 1 and 5, respectively.) The reader will note that our questions regarding the desirability of S-purposes and justness of actions are in essence the two questions, respectively.

[20] I borrow this somewhat saucy terminology from Hare, *Freedom and Reason,* pp. 157–87.

using a not-so-just means. With a shortage of cadavers for instructional use in medical schools, it might be deemed *very* desirable for the division of surgical instruction to obtain cadavers for class use. One can imagine quite convincing arguments to buttress the claim that obtaining the cadavers is desirable in the nth degree, e.g., think of the lives that over the span of the careers of the budding physicians could be saved or otherwise prolonged thanks to proper surgical instruction, for which cadavers are essential. Our fanatical utilitarian might point out that the S-purpose is so very desirable as to make the forced recruitment of those who are flunking out of medical school into the ranks of the cadaver corps a "justifiable" injustice.

Unfortunately, far more ordinary examples of the fanatical utilitarian's argument, if with less bizarre content, are to be found in the usual conduct of education. Take, for example, the case in which the whole class is "kept in after school" for the misdeed of one student, in order to make the recurrence of the misdeed less likely. The form of the argument is this: The disregard of principles that specify logical conditions for just action is acceptable if the S-purposes appear formidable enough. In order to disallow such a sleight of "moral mind" and to insist that justness is an *essential* feature of any morally justifiable policy, it is necessary to define principles of justice as being of a higher lexical order than any S-purposes, regardless of how good the S-purposes are judged to be.[21] Under this ruling, while S-purposes are "give-up-able," justness criteria for R-purposes are not. In other words, if no just means can be identified for achieving specified goals, then *no* policy may be better than any policy at all.

[21] For one oft-quoted statement of "the priority of justice over efficiency and welfare," see John Rawls, *Theory of Justice* (Cambridge, Mass.: Harvard University Press, 1971), pp. 302–3.

THE TOLERABILITY TEST

Once again we must face the question of whether the tests we have identified to this point are sufficient to distinguish justifiable policies. If a policy's purposes are desirable and if its means are both effective and just, must the policy be judged justifiable? On considering the following hypothetical case, the answer appears to be negative.

Imagine that an advocate of physical fitness proposes a state policy, the purpose of which is to make very likely *each* public school student's acquiring a wide range of individual skills that, if utilized, promote physical fitness. The prescribed means is to require through accreditation procedures that each school provide every student with daily access to the full range of gymnastic equipment, an Olympic regulation swimming pool, a gold course, a properly maintained running track, a bicycle, a bowling alley, an archery range, and a host of other individual sports facilities.

For the sake of this example, let us imagine that the goal is justifiable as an educational purpose and that the provision of such individual sports facilities is known (perhaps from a pilot study) to be effective as a means for making each student's acquisition of skills that can be used to promote a desirable level of physical fitness throughout adult life. Further, let us assume that the state superintendent's withholding accreditation from those schools that do not provide the sports facilities is not unjust. Although the policy might pass the first three tests of justifiability, to judge this policy justifiable would seem odd in view of the remarkably extravagant expenditure of schooling resources that it would demand. Even if we imagine that the cost of such sports facilities would not surpass the total budget of any school, we would likely think the costs of compliance with the policy too high for the policy to be justifiable—too high because to support such a policy would require a violation of curricular priorities. That is, we would not consider the policy unjustifiable because it costs x dollars, but because its costs are out of proportion.

To understand this fourth way in which an educational policy can fail to be justifiable, it is important to be clear about what it means for policy costs to be "out of porportion." First, suppose that Aesop's Grasshopper were to reveal that he considers both good food and frolicking to be *necessary* features of the Good Life. Were, then, the Grasshopper to decide to expend so much of his resources in frolicking that he would be unable to obtain good food, then he would have sacrificed an essential feature of the Good Life and so have lost it. Second, suppose that Simple Simon values literacy over going to fairs, but because he is easily confused about what he should be doing, he ends up having spent far more of his energies in going to fairs than in learning to read. It is the point *either* at which the pursuit of one essential element of the Good Life precludes the pursuit of another necessary feature *or* at which the pursuit of one element of the Good Life surpasses or does not measure up to its level of priority that we would say that its cost is out of proportion. Thus, to determine whether a policy costs too much, one must know more than a dollar figure. One must know how valuable the S-purpose is *in comparison* to the other S-purposes with which it is held in conjunction.

It is, I suspect, consideration of proportionality that commonly is lacking in the arguments of those who perennially propose, for example, that a barrage of new courses be tacked to curricula from elementary school through the university. Arguments in support of the proposed courses usually focus on the "absolute" importance of the subject matters, rather than their importance relative to other sub-

ject matters that compete for the same educational resources. Examples are easily found: the elementary school
curriculum advisers are told that each child should have a
year's course on good grooming "because it is important
that our children learn to look neat"; a secondary school curriculum board hears how important it is that high school
students be offered courses in "comparison shopping"; a
university curriculum committee is told of the importance
of approving a new interdisciplinary department of occult
studies. Frequently, when such proposals are turned down,
the negative vote is misinterpreted as a denial that mastery
or understanding of the subject matter in question has any
value whatsoever. And when such proposals are adopted
without consideration of proportionality, the results can be
catastrophic, e.g., a fifth-grade curriculum that includes but
two periods of English-language instruction per week. This
is not, of course, to say that changes in curricular or any
other kind of educational policy are never justifiable. Instead, the point here is that if a proposed policy is out of
proportion, then it is not justifiable.

In addition to being out of proportion, there is a second
sense in which a policy can cost too much to be justifiable.
Imagine that there is some policy, compliance with which
would be far less costly than going along with the proposed
sports-facility policy. Even if we were to have hypothesized
a policy that is proportional in the context of other concur-
rent S-purposes, if there were an alternative, less expensive
policy option which as well happened to pass the other three
tests of justification, the proposed policy would not be justifiable in the sense that it would not be the more rational of
the two choices.[22] If, then, we were to say that the fourth

[22] The point here regarding cost of means and the earlier
point pertaining to the effectiveness of means stand as the two

test of justifiability is that the costs of complying with the policy (A_i's actually X-ing whenever C obtains) must be acceptable, by this should be understood both (1) that the costs for pursuing the S-purpose are not out of proportion to the worth of the S-purpose relative to other desirable purposes; and (2) that the policy means is, ceteris paribus, the least costly of perceived alternatives.

To this point we have talked of costs only in terms of the required expenditure of resources. A second category of costs that would appear essential to a consideration of whether any particular policy is justifiable would consist of those perceived non-S results of "A's X-ing whenever C obtains" that are not desirable. Now it would be unrealistic to expect any single social action, much less any policy, to effect only S, that state of affairs which provides the point for making the policy. When one opens a door to admit a guest, a fly may come in. When one requires students to read a particular book or listen to a particular piece of music, they may learn to identify that piece of the culture (the S-purpose), but they may also come to dislike the book or music for its having been a required experience. Or, one may toil over Latin texts for the purpose of mastering Latin and be pleasantly surprised to find that a "side effect" was a greater mastery of English. That is, when we do X for the purpose of achieving S, S may result, but so may T, U, V, and W, some of which may be desirable and others of which may be undesirable, some of which we may have predicted and others of which may take us by surprise. Once any non-S effects of "A's X-ing whenever C obtains" are judged desirable, then they are irrelevant to a determination of whether the policy is justifiable, except perhaps when "all other things are equal" between two policy options and one

points on which considerations of rational choice as discussed in chapter 3 and justifiable action, the topic of this chapter, overlap.

has more desirable non-S results. But any undesirable non-S effects must always enter into the determination of whether the policy is justifiable.[23]

It is far easier to specify formally how a consideration of undesirable non-S results of "A's X-ing whenever C obtains" ought to enter into policy considerations than to carry out the actual "calculation" when trying to decide whether a particular policy is justifiable. First, let us turn to the formal point. The existence or likelihood of an undesirable non-S result does not necessarily make a policy unjustifiable. For example, the pain caused by a tetanus shot is surely tolerable when the achievable S-purpose for which that pain is suffered is the guarding of a person from the far more ominous prospect of contracting tetanus. And surely the discomfort of building up finger callouses in practicing the mandolin is tolerable when weighed against the skills in playing the mandolin that can be acquired only through practice. Clearly, undesirable "side effects" do not necessarily make a policy unjustifiable. If they are tolerable when weighed against the value of the S-purpose that the policy is designed to achieve, then the policy may still be justifiable.

But because we are commonly unable to assign exact values to the policy goal and other outcomes, in any actual case the calculation of whether the undesirable side effects are tolerable when weighed against the "main effect" S is not so straightforward. This is the practical point—a point that extends as well to the calculation of whether costs are in or out of proportion. And given that we may be unable to assign numerical utilities to elements of the Good Life, one may wonder whether it even makes sense to talk of calcu-

[23] To be sure, many "side effects" are unanticipated and so can hardly enter into a determination of whether a policy is justifiable. The point here is that when they are anticipated, they must be taken into consideration.

lating whether the non-S results of a policy are tolerable. Yet, unless we have some nonarbitrary basis for distinguishing between the value magnitude of the benefits and costs plus undesirable side effects, we cannot rationally answer the fourth test of justifiability and so cannot determine whether a policy is justifiable. I have no magic way out of this dilemma, but to suggest that in a *rough* way we are in fact able to assign values and "calculate" what in any case would constitute proportionality and a tolerable level of undesirable side effects. When, given the roughness of defined value magnitudes, the shots are too close to call, then it might make sense to say that the proposed policy is not clearly justifiable, but this does not necessarily mean that it should be given up. However, if one wished to "play it safe," then a search for another, stronger policy would seem warranted.

To recap, the point of the fourth test of justifiability, the tolerability test, is to determine whether the costs measured both in expenditure of resources and undesirable non-S-purpose results of "A's X-ing whenever C obtains" are tolerable. This test consists of three parts: a test of proportionality, a comparative-cost test, and a test for acceptability of undesirable side effects. To pass the test of proportionality, the resource costs of pursuing the policy's S-purposes must not be out of proportion to the worth of that S-purpose relative to other S-purposes also being pursued. The comparative-cost test specifies that both the resource costs and the undesirable-side-effect costs of the policy in question must be, ceteris paribus (here, all other tests having been passed), lower than those costs of any perceived alternative. According to the third test, any undesirable effects of "A's X-ing whenever C obtains" must be judged to be tolerable when weighed against the value of the S-purpose the policy is designed to achieve.

JUSTIFICATION THROUGH RATIONAL DISCOURSE

At the outset of this chapter it was noted that the point of concerning ourselves with the justification of policies as the giving of the right kind of supporting reasons was to try to uncover what must be true to say that we should support a policy choice. In response to that question we found that if a person is to believe on relevant grounds that a policy is justifiable, he must believe that the action it prescribes is just, that the purpose of that action is desirable, that the action is likely to effect that state of affairs that constitutes the purpose, and that the costs of the action in resources and undesirable side effects are tolerable. But, as the person who would reduce justification to partisan mutual adjustment without regard to grounds on which the policy is accepted or rejected would likely point out, to require that a policy be justifiable qua supportable on relevant grounds is not to ensure consensus. That is, any two persons may both have applied all the tests of justifiability to some policy only to arrive at contrary conclusions.

At this point the archetypal skip-the-nonsense skeptic would note that all our concern with the rational justification of educational policies has, alas, been in vain, for as we can clearly see, differences in view in the final analysis boil down to basic value differences that simply don't lend themselves to rational resolution. Further, so the argument would go, we might as well have skipped the tests of justification and have gone directly to some procedure for settling conflicts, e.g., swinging clubs, flipping coins, or voting. Our skeptic's assumption is, as we shall see, unwarranted. Contrary to what the skeptic claims, because two persons might apply the four tests of justifiability and still disagree as to whether the policy in question is justifiable, it does not necessarily follow that the two persons' basic values are in conflict. Instead, as is argued in this section, a difference in judgment deriving from these rational reflections on the justifiability of a policy occasions a continuation of the process of justification to a stage of rational *discourse*.

In order to identify what would constitute justification through rational discourse, we need first to demonstrate that from differences in properly tested opinions as to the justifiability of policies it does not necessarily follow that those differences derive from conflicts in basic values. For purposes of demonstration, let us consider a policy decision within a hypothetical, closed community which consists of persons who share the same cultural and ethnic pasts and who are of a single socioeconomic group and who share the same visions of the Good Life. Here, rather than tack on a number of other qualifiers, all of which would further distinguish the community as value-mono-lithic in the greatest conceivable degree, let us simply define this hypothetical community as one in which all basic values (social, moral, aesthetic and otherwise) are shared. If in this community both person A and person B apply the justness, desirability, effectiveness, and tolerability tests and if the respective A and B results of those tests disagree as to the justifiability of the policy in question, we cannot account for that disagreement by pointing to any basic value difference, for there is none. To flesh out this hypothetical case, imagine that someone has proposed that the community design an educational policy to promote the development of an excellent community-financed orchestra. More specifically, the proposed policy is annually to place all eight-year-olds whose verbal achievement is below some specified level in a special twelve-year school devoted exclusively to the development of musical skills and appreciation.

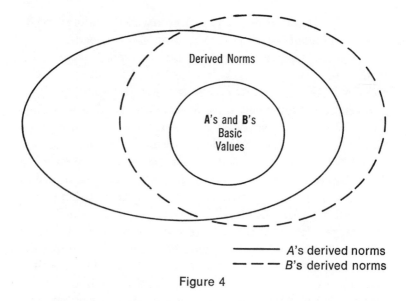

A's derived norms
B's derived norms

Figure 4

To see in what ways two persons who share the same basic values might disagree on whether a policy passes the tests of justifiability, let us consider how A and B might fail to get the same results on each test. It should, here, be borne in mind that only their results on one of the four tests need conflict for their evaluations of the policy to differ.

Consider first their applications of the desirability test. While both A and B may be said to place a high value on orchestral music in that both assign such music a central place in the Good Life, of the two only A finds the policy's goal of an excellent community-financed orchestra desirable. B, on the other hand, judges that S-purpose to be undesirable. Were B to request A to justify his claim that the S-purpose is desirable, A might appeal to the central role music plays in the Good Life, whereupon B would agree that such is the role of music. But B might go on to note that it is not just any central role of music that they mutually value, but more specifically music as it is voluntarily offered as a manner of avocation rather than vocation. Here B's point would be that A's description of the policy's S-purpose needs refinement if it is actually to be justifiable by appeal to A's own (and B's) values. A might respond that he had simply not thought about the way in which they valued music as carefully as had B, that B's point is a good one, and that the proposed policy does need to be radically reworked to be made justifiable. In other cases of disagreement on the desirability of S-purposes, A might have worked out a supportive argument that B had not thought of, but which B would find convincing were A to call it to his attention.

Much as A and B might share basic values and yet disagree on the desirability of a policy's S-purpose, so they might share basic values and disagree on the effectiveness of the proposed policy's means for achieving the S-purpose. This time, let the S-purpose be judged desirable by both A and B, and let us say that A's evidence that such a music education policy would likely result in an excellent professional community orchestra is a similar policy that has been producing excellent community orchestras in a community in another country. B disagrees with A's conclusion, for B sees differences between the two communities that suggest that the results would likely be different. For example, B points out, in the culture of the other community children are assigned professional roles early in life and are taught not to question their assignments, while in the culture of A and B's community, children are generally encouraged to delay decisions regarding to what professional roles they will aspire until they have reached majority. In the case of the effectiveness test, if A and B disagree, it would likely be over the relevance and soundness of the empirical evidence mustered in support of the claim that the proposed policy's means would effect the

S-purpose. As in the disagreement over the desirability of the policy's goal, once again the dispute is in theory resolvable by appeal to objective canons of criticism.

A similar point may be made about disagreement over whether a policy's means is just. In this case we can even allow A and B to share the same principles of justice and yet find them in conflict over whether the policy's action is just. Let us say, for purposes of the example, that both A and B share one formulation of Rawls's two principles of justice: [24] (1) "each person participating in a practice [here, a policy], or affected by it, has an equal right to the most extensive liberty compatible with like liberty for all"; and (2) "inequities are arbitrary unless it is reasonable to expect that they will work out for everyone's advantage and *provided the positions and offices to which they attach, or from which they may be gained, are open to all*" (italics added for this example).

Here A might judge the means to be just in that all seem to have access to the orchestra's positions by virtue of the fact that any child can have low verbal achievement. B, on the other hand, might judge the means unjust on the grounds that the manner in which the positions are open to all is not just in that the criteria for access are irrelevant and thus it may be said that those positions are *not* in fact open to all because they are not open to children with high verbal achievement. The point here is that while both A and B might assent to the same principles of justice, one may unknowingly *mis*apply those principles. Once again, the disagreement can be resolved by appeal to common rules of criticism. It might be noted that with regard to the justness test, rationally resolvable disagreement frequently occurs when one or more of the parties has not yet encountered or himself thought through a state-

[24] Rawls, "Justice as Fairness."

ment of principles of justice. In such cases, the person who is judging the justness of the policy's means has to rely on what "seems" just and so he may judge to be just those means which on further reflection he would deem unjust.

Perhaps the most common form of nonvalue difference in views of the justifiability of a policy comes when one party in the dispute thinks of undesirable side effects that simply had not occurred to the other. In the case of the music education policy, for example, A may have given the policy passing marks because he could think of no intolerable side effects that might result from the policy action. B predicted that such a policy might over time diminish the role of music in the community, a thesis for which he has some support. Since A also views the present role of music as essential to the Good Life, A would very likely change his view of the proposed policy on having the intolerable side effect called to his attention.

Parallel resolvable disagreements can be imagined that rest on the test of proportionality and the comparative-cost test, but let an example of a difference which derives from the test of proportionality suffice here. Let us say that A has become so enamored with the program of music education which the policy prescribes that he has lost sight of something he values even more than the envisioned role of music in community life. What A values, but temporarily is unable to see due to his enthusiasm for the music education policy, is a breadth of education that enables individuals to be "self-sufficient" in the making of "responsible personal and moral decisions."[25] On learning of A's support for the proposed policy, B (here played by Scheffler) reminds A of the supersedent value of the learner's

[25] This is a guiding principle for curriculum decisions that Israel Scheffler develops in brief form in "Justifying Curriculum Decisions," in *Reason and Teaching*, pp. 122–25. (Reprinted from *School Review* 66 [1958]: 461–72.)

attaining "self-sufficiency as [educationally] economically as possible," [26] and observes that music education to the exclusion of content with greater generalizability or "transfer" value would preclude pursuit of the self-sufficiency goal. Note that A need not alter a single value to withdraw his support of the proposed policy; he has only to allow himself the latitude of rational revisability of his judgments.

The striking feature of "justification through rational discourse," where differences are not value differences, is that it serves not only to encourage consensus on grounds as strong as any member of the community can muster, but also to *educate* those individuals who engage in the activity of rational discourse. Whatever the specific form of the test of justifiability that is being run, the acknowledgment of agreement is commonly of the form, "I just hadn't thought of it that way, but I must agree," or, "Not having articulated a principle of justice before, I guess my thinking was not as precise as it needed to be to see the difficulty with my policy proposal."

Here the skeptic might agree that justification through rational discourse appears to offer a promising route to rational consensus when everyone shares basic values, but might add that cases of differences of opinion that do not derive from value differences are rare. So, our skeptic would conclude, if rational justification has an educative function, it does not have wide applicability. My hunch is that even in the purportedly "culturally pluralistic" United States, the range of shared values is sufficient to make many differences of view regarding educational policies rationally resolvable. I suspect the reason that this most often does not appear to be the case is a general lack of analytic understanding of what policies are and what constitutes the tests of their justification. That is, while the

[26] Ibid., p. 123.

relevant public must, of course, share some values or norms if any policy is to be mutually justifiable, often lack of consensus derives not from disparate values, but from lack of analytic understanding of what constitutes rational justification of policies.

Though my view of the most common source of difficulties in justifying policies may be right, the skeptic's view is also right, at least to some extent. That is, some differences of opinion derive from basic value differences. Such differences can be viewed as rationally unresolvable differences of opinion regarding what constitutes a desirable effect (a benefit) of a policy action and what counts as a cost. The extent to which our skeptic is right is the extent to which policies must be justifiable by appeal to rock bottom values or initial commitments.[27] But because value differences may themselves not be rationally resolvable should not be mistaken to mean that if there are such basic value differences, mutually justifiable policies cannot be found. Where such value differences exist, rational justification could not proceed as described but would instead consist in the identification of policies that fall within the overlapping areas of derived norms—norms derived from the basic values.

For an example of mutually justifiable educational policies that might be said to be supportable by appeal to different basic values, consider these two justifications of an elementary-level curricular policy that centers on the "three Rs." The minister of education in the Soviet Union might perceive the point of education to be the creation of the "New Soviet Man." It is plausible that she might view mastery of a basic "three Rs" curriculum to be necessary to the development of persons toward this ideal image that

[27] I take the term "initial commitments" from Israel Scheffler, "On Justification and Commitment," *Journal of Philosophy* 51, no. 6 (18 March 1954): 180–90.

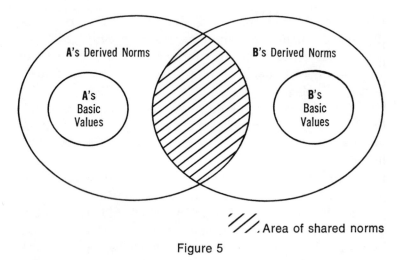

Figure 5

she and her fellow citizens prize. Likewise, an American educator might view a basic "three Rs" curriculum on the elementary level to be rationally justifiable because he believes that without a mastery of the "three Rs," a citizen would be unable to exercise his First Amendment rights. In such cases the policy is mutually and rationally justifiable, though by appeal to shared norms that derive from different basic values.

If we assume an analytic understanding of 'policy' and the rational justification of policies, our skeptic is correct in saying that differences of opinion over policies are rationally unresolvable only in those cases in which *neither* basic values *nor* derived norms are shared. Only when we fail to uncover any area of shared norms is the most rational way to arrive at policy decisions to employ immediately some sort of "settlement" procedure, e.g., balloting, to determine what ought to be done. Of course, to be just, that procedure would have to accord with some principles for the adjudication of conflicts that are deemed mutually acceptable by appeal to some rules of political enfranchisement and rights. This is to say, for *any* procedure for adjudicating rationally unresolvable differences to be nonarbitrary, the parties must share *some* rule of polity. When such a rule is not shared, then I suspect our skeptic is dead right: neither rational justification of policies nor rational settlement of differences of opinion is possible. That bleak picture, I would suggest, actually exists only when the basis of the polity, some form of government, has collapsed. Since the context in which educational policies are typically made is some polity, and insofar as the relevant public of any educational policy commonly shares a wide range of derived norms and even basic values to some extent, our skeptic's pessimism need not dash our hopes for creating rationally justifiable educational policies. Short of shared norms and values, we would have to turn to rational settlement through bartering within the rules of the polity.

SUMMARY

After dismissing the "politicking" and "selling" views of justification as unhelpful in any attempt to decide whether we *should* accept a particular educational policy choice, we addressed directly the question of what must be true to say that a policy choice is justifiable in the sense of being supportable on nonarbitrary grounds. In response, four necessary tests for justifiability were identified—tests that any educational policy would have to pass to be judged objectively justifiable. In the order of their presentation, those tests are as follows:

The desirability test. Weak form: the S-purpose of the educational policy must qualify as desirable on *some* defensible criteria; strong form (for *educational* justifiability): the S-purpose must promote or be constitutive of a developing of beliefs, attitudes, skills, dispositions, values, or tastes that are deemed conducive to or constitutive of the Good Life under some description.

The effectiveness test. "*A*'s *X*-ing whenever *C* obtains" must be more likely than any other perceived means, ceteris paribus (reference to justness test), to effect the *S*-purpose, if the *S*-purpose is achievable. If the *S*-purpose is unachievable, then "*A*'s *X*-ing whenever *C* obtains" must be more likely to effect a state of affairs that resembles the *S*-purpose more closely than any other perceived means.

The justness test. "*A*'s *X*-ing whenever *C* obtains" must be just. Or, alternatively, the *R*-purposes with which "*A*'s *X*-ing whenever *C* obtains" accords must be just.

The tolerability test. The costs measured both in expenditure of resources and undesirable results of "*A*'s *X*-ing whenever *C* obtains" must be tolerable, where tolerability is determined by three separate tests: the test of proportionality (the costs of "*A*'s *X*-ing whenever *C* obtains" must not be out of proportion to the worth of the *S*-purpose relative to other desirable purposes), the comparative-cost test ("*A*'s *X*-ing whenever *C* obtains" must be the least costly of perceived means that are otherwise acceptable), and the test for acceptability of undesirable side effects (any undesirable results of "*A*'s *X*-ing whenever *C* obtains" must be tolerable when weighed against the value of the *S*-purpose).

The order in which these tests were introduced is at variance with the order in which they would logically be applied in that the justness test was found to take precedence over the desirability test. Further, it should be noted that there would be no point in applying the effectiveness test and tolerability test if a policy did not pass the desirability test. The tests for justifiability would, then, logically be applied in this order: (1) the justness test, (2) the desirability test, (3) the effectiveness test, and (4) the tolerability test.

It was then noted that person A and person B might apply the tests for justification and yet disagree on the justifiability of a given policy. A view was presented that such a disagreement should occasion a second stage in the determination of whether a policy is justifiable, i.e., that the stage of rational reflection should, if disagreement ensues, be followed by a stage of rational discourse. If A and B share basic values, then rational consensus regarding the justifiability of the policy in question may be achieved by appealing to shared canons of rational criticism. If A and B share no basic values, then rational consensus regarding the justifiability of the policy may be achieved by locating and appealing to shared "derived" norms, as well as to canons of rational criticism. Only when no shared basic values and no areas of shared norms can be located (in any society, a highly unlikely state of affairs) would rational consensus on the justifiability status of a policy be impossible. Should there be no shared norms or values, rational settlement of conflicting views would be possible, but if and only if A and B agree to procedural rules. That is, rational settlement of such policy differences is possible only within a polity. In sum, if A and B have applied the four nonarbitrary tests for justifiability of educational policies and if A's test results differ from B's, we need *not* give up a search for rational consensus on whether the policy choice in question is justifiable.

FIVE

TOWARD SOUND EDUCATIONAL POLICY MAKING

WHEN ONE GOES TO the rapidly growing literature on policy, policy making, and the policy sciences, he or she is most commonly met with discussions of "processes": the policy process, the planning process, the policy-making process, the political process, and the like. Under these rubrics one finds descriptions of how policies are generally made, how planning in general is actually carried out, how policy making in fact proceeds, and so forth. Taken as accounts of "how policy is *actually* made," the adequacy of these descriptions rests, of course, on their empirical supportability. That is, whether the satisficing model, disjointed incrementalism, partisan mutual adjustment, or any other description jibes well with how policies are commonly made can be tested by empirical study. And, it should be noted, much as descriptions of traffic patterns and the eating or buying habits of a population can serve to inform us in our decisions regarding how we ought to route traffic and how we ought to alter our eating or buying habits, so descriptions of how policies are made can provide us with information that is requisite to making sound decisions on what we ought to be doing when making policies. In other words, a process description is a *description of behavior* and, as such, cannot itself recommend action; but it can provide information that is essential to coming to careful decisions about how policies *ought* to be made.

That process descriptions of educational policy making can, when considered along with other facts and norms, help us decide what to do is not at issue here. Rather, I wish to call attention to the potential and, I fear, common misuse of such descriptions of how policies are made. The problem I point to is a case of is-ought conflation, under which one takes what he ought to do directly from observations of how things are done. An academic philosopher might wince and note that Hume's dictum, what ought to be done cannot be derived from what is, should long ago have cleared up such confusions, at least in a general way. But even a casual collector of reasons policy makers (educational policy makers included) give for policy decisions would note that many decisions are made *as if* "ought" were deducible from "is."

One does not have to turn to "Watergate participants" for examples. When asked why he adopted a policy of "keeping in" during recess those students who miss x spelling words, a teacher responds, "That's the way it's done here," as if that were sufficient reason for deciding what *ought* to be done. When asked her reasons for voting against the state's funding of local schools, a legislator replies, "In this state, we finance schools through local property taxes." Frequently the is-ought conflation appears in another form: because policies *are* commonly made as knee-jerking responses, that is sufficient reason for one's thinking he *ought* to do the same. For example, a recent associate commissioner for Adult, Vocational, and Library Programs in the U.S. Office of Education remarked, "I don't sit down and determine policy. But on a pragmatic day-to-day response to problems, concepts emerge that taken together constitute policy. Policy and philosophy come after the fact." [1]

In the first four chapters of this book, my concern has been to develop a clearer understanding of what constitutes policy in general and educational policy in particular, what sort of rationality might be expected of policy choices and what would have to be true to say that an educational policy is justifiable. While I have maintained throughout that such considerations are essential to sound policy making, I have at every turn been haunted by a comment I have come to expect from my educator-students and colleagues. While the wording varies, the point of the comment, echoes of which never seem to fade away, is as follows: "All this talk about rationally justifiable policies makes sense, but it's pretty utopian. As makers of educational policies, our real concern is to keep the lid on, to keep things from flying apart, to maintain some semblance of order. Our real concerns are to survive and to cope. Any concern with justifiability must be treated as frosting, to be added if time and resources permit, which of course they never do." To the extent to which the existence of educational programs must rely on short-term grants, and in the degree to which educational policy making is embedded in unwieldy bureaucracies of massive proportions, a preoccupation with survival and coping to the exclusion of considerations of justifiability is understandable. But being an

[1] Norman C. Thomas, *Education in National Politics* (New York: David McKay, 1975), p. 124.

understandable approach to educational policy making does not make it a commendable one. Much as we can understand why persons in the Donner party turned to cannibalism, we can understand why educational policy makers might fail to consider the justifiability of policies they make and support. Sometimes conditions discourage our acting as we believe we ought. But adversity of conditions cannot make an uncommendable action commendable. While conditions might be hostile to commendable action, they cannot prevent commendable efforts.

Whether the source of this lack of universal concern with the justifiability of educational policies is the conflation of "is" and "ought" or a preoccupation with surviving and coping, a shrug of shoulders and sigh of "oh, well" is most inappropriate. If as educational policy makers we are to act defensibly, then we must act mindfully; we must become concerned with the justifiability of every educational policy choice. To demand anything less than defensible choices from educational policy makers is to assent to shoddy educational policies—policies without which education would likely fare better.

The point here is not that no choice is defensible if it is not justifiable. Indeed, most of us allow ourselves a range of personal choices which we base on whim or at least unexamined grounds, e.g., whether to order Swiss on rye or pumpernickel or whether to buy red or yellow laces for our hiking boots. We say that the unjustifiable choice of rye over pumpernickel is defensible because whichever we choose does not matter. Policy choices do matter. If they did not, there would be no point in making a policy. Further, it might be argued, any *social* policy choice affects more than the policy maker and so by its social nature must be justifiable to be defensible.

There is an alternative way to make this point. To observe that an educational policy *can* be made without serious regard to its justifiability is no grounds for claiming that concerns with justifiability ought not to be taken seriously. That people can function as educational policy-making hacks (and collect paychecks) constitutes no good reason for their doing so. Given a choice between systematic education governed by policies that are not considered justifiable and no systematic education at all, the wiser choice would surely be the latter. Here I find myself arguing such an obvious point that I am almost embarrassed. Yet, as I look about, I wonder if the point is really all that obvious.

If educational policy makers neither act as if they are deducing an "ought" from an "is" nor consider justification merely an optional concern, there is still no assurance (even if we assume a beneficent intent) that they will make educational policies that match their level of understanding of sound policy making. That is, even if a person understood the concept of policy (chapter 1) and the notion of educational policy (chapter 2), the elements of rational policy choices (chapter 3) and the tests of justifiability for educational policies (chapter 4), when setting out to make sound educational policies he might still fail, not because the world may refuse to cooperate, but because he fails to employ what he knows or understands. My concern here is not to develop a theory of applied epistemology or a theory for the psychology of the application of knowledge (though those are intriguing invitations). Rather, my concern is to suggest some points that, if borne in mind, might assist the educational policy maker, who already has acquired an analytic understanding of educational policy and its justification, in applying what he already knows about sound policy making.

An analogy may help to clarify what I propose as the program for this chapter. When writing in a language other than one's own, a person often makes errors that he could correct on the basis of his present knowledge of that second language *if only* he were to "catch" the errors. Whether a person writes well or poorly in that language, then, depends on not only what he knows of the language but also the routines or strategies that he uses to check himself. The writer who systematically goes back over his work with categories of potential errors in mind (e.g., for nouns, the categories of declension, case, gender, and number) is more likely to spot errors. If we can make explicit those categories of errors or ways in which educational policy making can fail to be sound, then we will have a way of checking our policy-making attempts to see that they are as sound as we know how to make them. Such a set of error categories can best serve, then, not as a recipe but as a check list.

After having identified a way to "correct" our educational policy-making tries, we turn to a second means for improving the application of our understandings of educational policy. It seems fairly safe to claim that around every activity of a society a body of "common sense" and folklore arises that affects the way in which persons engage in that activity. Seemingly inevitably, at least part of that folklore consists of fallacies. If these fallacies go undetected they can, as part and parcel of the beliefs on which we base policy decisions, lead to faulty policies. By identifying some of the more common fallacies that undergird the making of educational policy and by proposing principles which might be used to counter those fallacies, we will introduce educational policy makers to a second way to come closer to that degree of soundness of policy making of which they are, given what they know and understand, capable.

Finally, continuing in our effort to enable educational policy makers to make the quality of their educational policies commensurate with their understandings, we will survey some policy-making conditions that typically impede the considerations that sound educational policy making entails. By making note of the troublesome conditions, we can identify policy-making conditions that the educational policy maker should be concerned to improve.

CHECK LIST

It is important from the outset to be clear about the uses and limits of a check list. First, a check list cannot provide sufficient information to serve as a set of instructions, but it can serve to remind us to take into account some things that we know ought to be taken into account. For example, the check lists that NASA employed in the moon shots could not have served as a set of instructions on how to build and successfully launch a spaceship. Much less could the check list recommend whether one ought to try to send people to the moon. Instead, the NASA check lists served to remind technicians to check to see if particular parts of the system were functioning as they understood that they ought to be functioning for a proper liftoff and flight. Likewise, the check list that an educational policy maker might employ can serve neither to tell the policy maker whether he should be attempting such a policy nor to embellish his understanding of educational policy. Rather, a check list for sound educational policy making should be expected only to remind the policy maker to be sure to consider a particular set of points that careful reflection would tell him need to be taken into account— reflection on what he already understands about educational policy and the enterprise of policy making.

Second, if all points "check out" there is still no assurance that the policy maker has created a "flawless" educational policy. Things still might go wrong, especially in those aspects of policy making that are beyond the understanding of the particular policy maker or the reach of the particular check list. Much as on occasion NASA has declared that all systems read "Go" and yet the mission failed, a policy maker might exhaust the check list with positive responses and later, in retrospect, decide that the policy was for some reason not a prudent, efficacious, or judicious choice. That is to say, while a check list can help us apply our knowledge and understanding to our actions, the check list itself cannot guide us to more ingenious, wiser, and more humane actions than our knowledge and understanding can support (though sometimes we do have a stroke of luck).

Third, a check list might best be conceived of as an aid in looking for trouble. In essence, a check list provides us with some questions that, because of both their general applicability and their focus on necessary features of sound policy making, can call our attention to ways in which our attempts might fall short of sound educational policy making. Thus, to apply a check list properly one must *want* to find any weak spots, rather than to undertake an ego-saving or otherwise uncritical whitewash.

The Point and Rules of Educational Policy Making

The first cluster of questions on our check list serves to remind us of the point of making any such policy as we have in mind and the context of restraints within which we must attempt to achieve whatever our goal or goals. Were policy making an arbitrary game, such as chess, in which we may or may not choose to engage, then our check list would consist of questions exclusively from this cluster. That is, before engaging in an arbitrary game such as chess, one would want to remind himself that the point of that game (pleasure aside) is to capture his opponent's king and that the rules which must be followed while doing so are. . . . Though educational policy making is not "played" within the confines of a fully specified set of rules and though the point of any case of educational policy making is not arbitrarily specified, as any other purposive activity it is game-resembling in that it must have a point if it is to be done intelligently, and it must be done within the contextual restraints if it is to be done legitimately or acceptably. The first check-list question, then, reminds us that in making an educational policy we are trying to bring about some educationally justifiable state or states of affairs (S-purposes):

> 1.1. *What is the educational S-purpose (or purposes) of making this policy?*

Recall, here, from chapters 2 and 4 that to be an educationally justifiable S-purpose, the purpose must promote or be constitutive of persons' developing some beliefs, attitudes, skills, dispositions, values, understandings, or tastes (or any combination of these) in whatever direction or directions are deemed conducive to or constitutive of the Good Life under some description. The second question reminds us that policies are not made in a state of free suspension, but must be made within contextual restraints:

> 1.2. *What are the R-purposes that this policy must satisfy?*

R-purposes, it should be recalled, can derive from the political, moral, and institutional contexts of the given case of policy making. If, for example, the policy in question regards access to and maintenance of student records, then one set of restrictive rules would be found in the federal law that pertains to student records, for it is within that law that the student-records policy would be nested. From this example we can see that at least some R-purposes could be found by examining laws that one would not wish to violate in making the policy:

> 1.2.1. *What are the laws that "cover" policies of this content?*

A second set of R-purposes might be unearthed first by identifying what type of educational policy is in question (curricular, methodological, resource, or distributional) and then by identifying "higher level" or more outer policies of like kind. If, for example, one is concerned with making some classroom curricular policy, then it would likely be nested in a district curricular policy which, in turn, is nested in a state curricular policy. If we remember (from chapter 2) that when policy A is nested in policy B, B either restricts or expands the range of admissible policy As, then we can see that one source of R-purposes for the classroom curricular policy may well be those curricular policies within which it is nested. This brings us to an additional check-list question:

> 1.2.2. *If the policy is to be nested in another educational policy, what* R-*purposes do the more outer policies impose?*

A third set of R-purposes is found in the principles of just action and might be stated simply, if sweepingly, as follows:

> 1.2.3. *What are the rules or principles for just action?* [2]

---

[2] Whether one should ask the question using 'rules' or 'principles' for just action would depend upon one's position in the debate in moral philosophy over *act* and *rule* utilitarianism (otherwise called *extreme* and *restricted* utilitarianism). For one discussion of the distinction between moral rules and moral principles, see Marcus G. Singer, "Moral Rules and Principles," in *Moral Education,* ed. Barry I. Chazan and Jonas F. Soltis (New York: Teachers College Press, 1973). (Reprinted from *Essays in Moral Philosophy,* ed. A. I. Meldon [Seattle: University of Washington Press, 1958].)

The Justifiability of the Policy Candidate

The second cluster of questions on our check list reminds us that regardless of the merits of what we are in general attempting to achieve through systematic education, for educational policy making to be sound *each* policy must itself be rationally justifiable. For purposes of clarity of presentation, here I have separated the point and rules of making the policy from the justifiability of that policy, but one could insist with good reason that the first cluster of check-list questions is really a subset of the second. Clearly, the point of attending to S-purposes and R-purposes is to question the justifiability of the policy. Indeed the point of bothering with a check list at all is to try to make policies that are justifiable. This particular check-list organization need not present any difficulties if we bear in mind that there is overlap between the clusters and that the point of our constructing a check list is to encourage us to make policies as sound and soundly as we know how. In rough terms, then, for an educational policy to be justifiable, it must be both rational (chapters 3 and 4) and normatively justifiable (chapter 4). "Rational" is to be understood as at least perceived effective as a means (X-C) for achieving our policy purposes; by "normatively justifiable" is meant (1) that the educational purposes are supportable by appeal to some defensible view of the Good Life or norms derived therefrom and (2) that the policy means (X-C) for achieving those purposes are just.

Let us turn first to the requirement that the policy means be effective.

2.0. *Is X-C effective as a means for achieving the S-purpose?*

I trust that it is obvious that for a policy to be effective it must be "implementable." That is, the implementing agent

(A_i) must in fact be able to do X whenever C obtains. Typically, when someone proposes a policy that clearly could not, for whatever reason, be implemented, we say that the proposal is not feasible. If a policy is infeasible, it is ineffective in at least one way. For example, consider the imaginary case of a teacher who decides to adopt a policy of spending an hour each day with each student individually for some educational purpose. If the teacher has more students than working hours in the day, his policy could not possibly be effective in that it cannot be implemented.[3] Let, then, the first effectiveness item regard feasibility:

2.1. *Is it in fact possible for the implementing agent (*A_i*) to do* X *whenever* C *obtains?*

Second, if a means is to be effective it must be practical, i.e., conditions C must occur with sufficient frequency that the doing of X can effect S. For illustration, Ausubel's discussion of learning by discovery comes to mind.[4] If one were to try to teach a particular science curriculum by having the student make specified sorts of observations whenever the conditions are "right" for a discovery, then the policy would likely be ineffective in that the discovery conditions would likely *not* occur with sufficient frequency to allow the student to learn even a small piece of the basic curriculum within the course of a whole lifetime. We should, then, add a second effectiveness question to the check list—a question that regards practicality:

2.2. *Is* C *likely to recur with sufficient frequency for* A_i*'s* X-*ing whenever* C *obtains to effect the* S-*purpose?*

[3] For a discussion of implementation success, see Donna H. Kerr, "The Logic of 'Policy' and Successful Policies," *Policy Sciences* 7 (1976), in press.

[4] David P. Ausubel, "Learning by Discovery: Rationale and Mystique," *Bulletin of the National Association of Secondary School Principals* 45, no. 1 (1961): 18–58.

Perhaps the conceptually most central effectiveness question probes the grounds on which the policy maker is claiming that the means $(X\text{-}C)$ is likely to effect S:

2.3. *What basis do we have for the claim that A_i's X-ing whenever C obtains is likely to effect S?*

Clearly there are no assurances. Even a policy built on a very strongly supportable claim that $X\text{-}C$ is very likely to effect S might fail. The point, though, is that policies that are founded on flimsy or unsupportable claims are, generally speaking, not sound policies. If the policy maker has not already done so before turning to this check list, this question should send him scurrying for confirming (or disconfirming) evidence. A companion question asks us to consider not whether $X\text{-}C$ is likely to effect S, but whether another means, ceteris paribus, is more likely to do so:

2.4. *Is X-C the most likely of perceived means to effect S?*

There are cases, it should be noted, the nature of which call into question the very form of the central effectiveness question. As stated, item 2.2 appears to suggest that to be effective a policy must bring about state-of-affairs S. But such is not so for all cases of effective policies. On remembering that some educationally justifiable S-purposes are by nature unachievable (chapter 2), why logically we should not always expect S to be brought about becomes clear. The point here is that for policies with unachievable purposes we must pose slightly though significantly different effectiveness questions 2.2, 2.3, and 2.4. In each case S should be understood as S^*, a state of affairs that is closer to S than the present state of affairs. The point of 2.4, then, would be twofold: *both* to check the relative likelihood that

alternative means X-C would effect S* *and* to check the
likelihood that alternative X-C means would effect S**, a
state of affairs that resembles S more closely than S*.

My suspicion is that the above questions which regard
the effectiveness of the policy candidate as an instrument
for achieving some goal or goals are not crucial to a policy-
maker's check list in that the policy maker would take those
considerations into account anyway. If we take as crucial to
a check list any sort of consideration that is likely to be
overlooked, the most crucial items would surely be those
questions that pertain to the justifiability of the policy to
the relevant public—questions that go beyond "will it
work?" For openers, the policy maker would clearly need
to know:

3.1. *Who constitutes the relevant public for the suggested policy?*

Here it should be recalled from chapter 2 that the relevant
public, in any policy case, consists not only of those persons who are affected by A's doing X whenever conditions C
obtain, but also of those persons who can effect conditions
C under which A is obligated to do X. But merely to know
who composes the relevant public does not itself tell us
whether a particular policy is justifiable to that public. Further, for the policy to be justifiable in an objective rather
than just politicking or selling sense (chapter 4), it must
be justifiable on nonarbitrary grounds. That is, for a policy to
be justifiable in the stronger sense that we seek, it must be
more than merely acceptable to the relevant public. It must
be acceptable *on appropriate grounds*.

One of those appropriate considerations pertains to the
educational S-purposes of the policy as identified at the
outset of the check list. If the policy maker has in mind
particular educational S-purposes for the proposed policy,

those S-purposes are not necessarily justifiable to the relevant public. The policy maker must further query:

> 3.2. *Are the educational S-purposes of the proposed policy justifiable by appeal to basic values of the members of the relevant public?*

Or:

> 3.2′. *If the educational S-purposes of the proposed policy are not justifiable by appeal to basic values of any of the members of the relevant public, are then those S-purposes justifiable by appeal to norms that are derivable from their respective basic values?*

If neither question 3.2 nor 3.2′ can be answered affirmatively, it should then be remembered that the proposed policy is not justifiable no matter how sure and ingenious "*A*'s *X*-ing whenever *C* obtains" might be as an instrument for achieving the S-purposes.

So if members of the relevant public are "covered" by affirmative answers to 3.2 and 3.2′, then we are warranted in saying that the policy's S-purposes are justifiable, but we do not yet have warrant to claim that the policy is justifiable to the relevant public in that the *X-C* means may not be justifiable. One popular though potentially misleading way in which this same point is often made is by noting (when a policy which has justifiable ends has unjustifiable means), "That's just another case of the ends justifying the means!" On the misleading reading, the implicit false suggestion here is that a policy can be justified without justifiable ends.[5] More precisely and less misleadingly, the point is that justifiable ends are alone not sufficient to justify policies. It is to one of the remaining components that also are

[5] My thanks to Robert E. Tostberg for calling this misleading reading to my attention.

necessary to a sufficient set of justifying conditions that
the next check-list question calls our attention:

>   3.3. *Does "A's X-ing whenever C obtains," as
>   specified by the proposed policy,* not *violate
>   the relevant public's principles for just
>   action?*

Now it might seem that if we are confident that a
policy's S-purposes are desirable in the view of the relevant
public and that the policy's means (*A*'s *X*-ing whenever *C*
obtains) are just, then we must be confident that the policy
is justifiable to that public. But such is not necessarily the
case. At least four other conditions must obtain for the
policy to count as justifiable. It is from these conditions that
the last of this cluster of check-list questions derives. To
establish the first of these, it should be recalled that restrictive purposes (*R*-purposes) include, but are not limited to, rules or principles for just action. For example,
when policy *A* is embedded in policy *B* (chapter 2), the
S-purposes of *B* define at least some of the *R*-purposes of *A*.
That is, whatever constitutes the policy-*A* means, it must
be such that while achieving policy *A*'s S-purposes it does
not work counter to the S-purposes of policy *B*. Such restrictions as the S-purposes of the more outer policies can
restrict the range of admissible means and so count as
R-purposes. Thus, whenever the proposed policy would, if
adopted, be embedded in another existing policy or policies
which the relevant public finds justifiable on appropriate
grounds, *either* the proposed policy means must not violate
the *R*-purposes that the more outer policies impose *or* the
S-purposes of the proposed policy must override those of the
existing policies in which it *seemed* to be embedded. Here I
use "seemed" advisedly, for if the latter is the case, then it
is *not* the proposed policy that would be embedded in the
existing one, but the contrary, in which case the existing

policy may lose its justifiability status. Thus we can limit our statement of the check-list item to the former as follows:

    3.4. *Does the proposed policy violate any* R-*purposes that any more outer existing policies impose?*

A second quesion that must be answerable negatively for the proposed policy to count as justifiable to the relevant public is found in the first tolerability test, i.e., in the test of proportionality. Restated as a check-list question, that test becomes:

    3.5. *According to the basic values and derived norms of the relevant public, are the costs of "A's X-ing whenever C obtains" out of proportion to the worth of the proposed policy's S-purposes relative to other purposes that are justifiable by appeal to the basic values and derived norms of the relevant public?*

That is, a policy that passes the other check-list items may still fail to be justifiable in that the cost of its implementation would be out of proportion. From chapter 4 recall the case of the extravagant physical education policy that, though flawless in other respects, was not justifiable because its implementation would have prevented the pursuit of other equally as important or more important curricular purposes.

Another check-list item is lodged in the second tolerability test, the comparative-cost test. Restated as a check-list item which requires an affirmative response for us to pass on the policy, it reads:

    3.6. *Given the basic and derived norms of the relevant public, is "A's X-ing whenever C obtains" the least costly of perceived means that are otherwise justifiable?*

There are two ways to underscore the importance of this check-list item. First, if a policy is, ceteris paribus, not the least costly of the perceived alternatives it is not a rational choice and, hence, not justifiable.[6] Second, if a proposed policy would cost more than is deemed necessary, then the pursuit of other defensible purposes is hindered; thus the proposed policy would not be justifiable for it would require unnecessary cost to other human enterprises.

The last check-list item of the justifiability cluster is found in the third tolerability test, the test for acceptability of side effects. It reminds us both to try to determine what other than S is likely to be brought about by A's X-ing under C and to decide whether such side effects, if they are themselves undesirable, are tolerable:

> 3.7. *In a consideration based on the values and derived norms of the relevant public, if there are any anticipated undesirable side effects of "A's X-ing whenever C obtains," are those side effects tolerable when weighed against the S-purposes of the proposed policy?*

This check-list question reminds us not to become so enamored with the goodness of our intent and the justness of our planned action that we overlook the problems that our proposed action might create. Now some might object that it is impossible to assign exact values to states of affairs, whether goals or anticipated side effects and, therefore, that it is impossible to "weigh" undesirable outcomes against the desirable ones. As was granted in chapter 4, such calculations are necessarily rough, but a rough calculation is clearly better than no estimate at all. In cases in which we cannot say whether the answer to question 3.7 is yes or no,

---

[6] This is *not* to say that the least costly policy is necessarily the most rational. *'Ceteris paribus'* is crucial here.

then the point in pursuing the policy as proposed may be lost.

The Conduct of Rational Discourse

In order to get clear about why it is what we ought to include items on the educational policy-maker's check list that pertain to the conduct of rational discourse with the proposed policy as the topic, it is helpful to recall two distinctions. The first is a distinction between a policy's being *justified* and its being *justifiable*. The second is between a policy's being justifiable on *just some grounds* and its being justifiable on *appropriate grounds*.

If a policy's being justifiable to the relevant public were all that sound policy making required, then we would do best to hire philosophers or other persons who are clever thinkers to figure out some way to justify the policy in question by appealing to the relevant public's shared basic values or the norms derived therefrom and to skip the talk. Any cries of protest under this scheme would properly be dealt with by responding that if the public were as clever, they too would see how it is that the various policies are justifiable. Even if we were to require that the philosopher-policy makers adopt only those policies that are justifiable on the most stringent of grounds as defined by the established canons of criticism, we would still question the soundness of such cases of policy making.

We would question such cases of policy making on two grounds, empirical and moral. The empirical point would be that even though a policy might in fact be justifiable to the relevant public, if the relevant public has not properly "thought it through," then at best they cannot know whether the policy in question is justifiable and so they may have no reason in particular to comply with that policy, much less to act so as to enhance the chances of the policy's attaining its purposes. That is, a policy may well be undermined if the relevant public does not actually come to view the policy as justifiable. The moral point derives either from a view of the Good Life or from a view of what is right or just. A description of the Good Life to which I refer includes a claim to the effect that if a person is in some way affected by a policy and if that policy is justifiable (i.e., *can* be justified) to that person, a better state of affairs exists when that person in fact sees the policy as justifiable than when it is justifiable by appeal to his values but he does not so view it. The sort of description of just action to which I refer here would include a claim to the effect that if a person is able to understand an action which affects him as justifiable, mutatis mutandis, then that action is just only if (presumably through some form of rational discourse) that person comes to so view the action.

Rational discourse, then, appears to be an essential ingredient of sound policy making whenever any members of the relevant public do not from the outset view the proposed policy as justifiable. The point of rational discourse as a necessary feature of sound policy making is (1) to account for the initial disagreement (errors in reasoning, failure to take particular crucial matters into consideration, etc.) and (2) to attempt to arrive at agreement on the justifiability status of the policy through application of the established canons of criticism. Let the check-list items in this cluster be stated thus:

4.0. *Does the relevant public see the proposed policy as justifiable by appeal to their shared basic values or norms derived therefrom?*

4.1. *If the answer to question 4.0 is negative, has rational discourse been conducted?*

4.2. *If rational discourse has been conducted, have the bases of the initial disagreement been identified?*

4.3. *If the bases of initial disagreement have been identified, have the established canons of criticism been followed in the conduct of the discourse?*

FALLACIES AND ANTIDOTES

At this point (or even at the conclusion of chapter 4), on the basis that we have covered at least to some extent all the logical terrain of sound educational policy making, we could terminate this discussion. One appropriate concluding remark would suggest that in order to make policies sound and soundly one needs somehow to take into account "all of the above." I believe this to be true, but not too helpful. The fact is that when one is trying to formulate and criticize policies, "all of the above" must compete with previously acquired beliefs, some of which are likely not to be consistent with "the above." In other words, understanding the components of educational policy and sound policy making is one matter; bringing that understanding to bear in the formulation and criticism of policies is another.

The point of this section is twofold: (1) to identify some of the more salient fallacious beliefs that have grown up about educational policy making and with which our warranted beliefs must compete, and (2) to note some principles that might be held in mind to serve as antidotes to the respective fallacies. Of course there are no guarantees, but it does seem that we are more likely to make educational policies more soundly if we have identified those fallacies that are common to the enterprise of educational policy making. And here it is important to underscore that our concern is with *fallacies* rather than false statements and with *antidotes* rather than true statements. That is, we will focus not on just any false statements that could be made about sound policy making, but in particular on those that form the propositional core of mistaken ideas in accordance with which educational policy makers and their critics have been known to make and criticize policies. Likewise, we will focus not just on any true statement that could be made about sound policy making, but in particular on those principle-statements, the propositional cores of which counter those of the corresponding fallacies.

The Do-Something Fallacy

Whether teacher, legislator, librarian, school board member, or principal, every educational policy maker is familiar with the call for action in the waning hours of meetings of policy-making bodies. The plaint of a weary member *A* is that the policy-making body has done enough talking and that it is time to decide. If some member *B* objects on the grounds that they have not collected the information and considered those issues that need to be considered in order to be clear about the justifiability of the policy in question, *A* rejoins, "I know, I know; but we have to do something. This is an important problem!" In this scenario the conflict is over whether to give up immediate adoption of any policy for purposes of getting clear as to whether the proposed policy is justifiable (member *B*'s position) or whether to give up testing the proposed policy for justifiability in order to "take action now" (member *A*'s position).

To be sure, other cases occur in which the point of a call for action may be to draw attention to the fact that the justifiability tests have been run and that indeed it is time to act. But here let us focus on those instances in which the call for action is based on someone's wanting the policy-making body to *do something* (i.e., to adopt the proposed policy) *without regard to its justifiability.* While we might feel empathetic to *A*'s weariness and loss of patience, we should not think his reasoning defensible, for it is grounded on a fallacy.

This might be labeled the do-something fallacy, for at its core is the mistaken belief that a concern with adopting some policy takes precedence over all other considerations. A correlative mistaken belief is that a concern with the justifiability of the policy, one of the "other considerations," is give-up-able. If there is anything that follows from earlier chapters it is this: if policy making is to be sound, then carrying out the tests of justifiability cannot be given up unless the whole policy-making enterprise is to be abandoned as mindless. While one might assent to the principle that *justification is not give-up-able,* the principle that counters the do-something fallacy, anyone who has ever actually made policies recognizes that the temptations to violate that principle can be numerous and difficult to resist. Elected officials know that painstaking care to probe the justifiability of a policy proposal commonly has little effect on voter support. Teachers know that others' evaluation of their teaching typically is not founded on the soundness of the teachers' reasons for adopting classroom policies that give form and content to education in the classroom. School administrators know that how seriously they take policy decisions rarely affects community support. And so on. Rewards generally are for "producing" rather than for properly thinking through what to do. But that lamentable state of affairs cannot make the do-something fallacy any less fallacious.

The Magic Fallacy

If one were to look for a fallacy that has done perhaps the most to damage the reputation of public schooling, without much of a search one would find the magic fallacy. A scenario that provides the opportunity for application of this fallacy typically develops in this way. First, it is remarked that persons who are or ever have been of school age have a great number and variety of problems: some cannot read "up to grade level," some cannot find a job, some can find a job but not a lucrative one, some do not know how to balance a checkbook, some do not know what constitutes a balanced diet, some do not know what the Bill of Rights is, some do not know what to do with their leisure time, some have not acquired "good work habits," some do not know what methods of birth control are available, and so forth. For a second step in the development of the scenario, it is opined that the schools are not doing their job and rhetorically it is asked, "What are schools for if they do not serve to prevent people from having these problems?" Or, sometimes the scenario develops as a lament that the schools are not solving community or social problems, rather than problems of individuals.

Whichever way it unfolds, the line of reasoning contains a fallacious premise. This is the magic fallacy and it has two layers. The top layer of the fallacy is that for every problem there is a possible school policy. The bottom, less specific layer is that for every problem there is a policy.[7] Another way to describe this view might be to draw an analogy between what a magician appears to do and what an educator is expected to do. Much as every time a ma-

[7] This is how Nathan Glazer characterizes the liberal stance in "The Limits of Social Policy," *Commentary* 52, no. 3 (September 1971): 51.

gician wants a rabbit, all he appears to do is to reach into his black silken tophat, so whenever the public of the public schools perceive a problem, they expect those who make schooling policies to pull a solution in the form of a policy out of the educational tophat. And much as the audience would hiss and boo if the magician were to fail to appear to produce a rabbit, so they jeer when the schools fail to appear to produce policy solutions to perceived problems. Whence the name, the *magic* fallacy.

Here it is instructive to ask what would have to be true for it to be reasonable, correct, and otherwise appropriate for the public to await schooling policies for the solution of social ills and individual problems? Minimally, those persons who make schooling policies would have to have at their disposal resources and technology (broad sense) that would be adequate to the tasks at hand. Moreover, those policy makers would have to have control over all the variables that can determine such outcomes as, for example, who finds what job and how much he is paid. (Note that the schooling policy maker in this example would have to be able to control at least both the world economy and fate. Whether we would want to allow schooling policy makers such sweeping power is another question.) With regard to the bottom layer of the magic fallacy, for it to be true that every problem has a policy solution, those variables would have to be controllable not only in theory but also in practice, given our present state of knowledge and resources. Lest the wildness of that expectation be less than blatant, consider what an absurdity it would have been to expect the medical community to adopt policies to eradicate polio prior to the development of the Salk vaccine. Especially in those instances in which we know that we do not know enough to make policies intelligently, educational or otherwise, *no* policy would likely be a better bet than one based on wild guesses with an overlay of faked confidence.

To counter the magic fallacy, then, both policy maker and critic would do well to remind themselves of the principle that *not every problem has a policy solution* and, more particularly, not every problem has a schooling policy solution. What makes the magician's trick so spectacular is that he does not even need to have pieces of rabbits, much less a knowledge of their anatomy, to appear to produce them. He seems simply to do it. Presto. Unless we are willing to tolerate sleight-of-hand education (education that is not really so but only appears to be so), then we must expunge the magic fallacy from the set of beliefs on which we formulate and criticize educational policies.

The Fallacy of the Wise Slug

Commonly educational policy makers review existing policies to determine whether they should be revised. At the end of a segment of a school year, for example, a teacher may reconsider his methodological policies for purposes of determining whether the policies are achieving the desired results in acceptable ways. If his policies are not doing the job he expects of them, he wonders how they might be revised so as to improve them. Sometimes, unfortunately, he finds that his policies have failed miserably, but at other times they seem to be getting almost exactly the intended results. Whether the policy under review turns out to have been a total fiasco or a brilliant success, there is a piece of folklore which says that to proceed slowly is to proceed surely, wisely. This particular piece of policy-making folklore has recently been buttressed in the literature on social policy making by the view that the proper way to go about making policy decisions is to use the strat-

egy of "disjointed incrementalism." [8] The central identifying feature of that strategy of policy making is that one
limits the region of the policy proposals to those policies that
would effect states of affairs that differ only incrementally
from the status quo.[9] (It might be noted here that what
is called the strategy of disjointed incrementalism functions as a restrictive principle or R-purpose in the making
of any policy in that it restricts the range of allowable
policy candidates.) Whether one is pointing to the folk
wisdom that to proceed wisely one must proceed slowly
or to the more recent and now fashionable "disjointed incrementalism," one has located what I call the fallacy of the
wise slug.

To understand how it is that the fallacy of the wise
slug qualifies as a fallacy, it is important to identify more
precisely the false statement. It can be put in at least two
ways. First, if a policy is sound, it necessarily effects a new
state of affairs that is only slightly or incrementally different from that of the status quo. Just how different S' might
be from S is never made clear, but it could not be radically
different. Second, if it is true that some case of policy making is sound, it must be true that the policy maker does not
count as a serious policy candidate any policy that would
effect any state of affairs which differs more than slightly
or incrementally from the status quo.

To demonstrate that these statements, which I take
to say the same thing, are fallacious, let us return to the
example of the instructor who recognizes that his first-
term methodological policies for the teaching of reading,
say, have been stupendous failures. Not only have the students' reading-achievement scores dropped markedly, but

[8] David Braybrooke and Charles E. Lindblom, *A Strategy of
Decision: Policy Evaluation as a Social Process* (New York: Free
Press, 1963).
[9] Ibid., pp. 85–86.

also the students have begun to dislike reading anything whatsoever. All indicators suggest that what is needed is a policy that will alter radically (not in small increments) the status quo. That is, slowly and "wisely" to putter about with decreasing the degree of failure would be neither rational nor moral. Thus, playing the part of a wise slug in such circumstances would not constitute sound policy making. The wisdom of action-with-caution could perhaps be retained while the fallacy of the wise slug would be countered, if the policy maker were to adopt the *principle of maximum justifiable change*. According to this principle it is appropriate *not* to disallow categorically policy candidates that would effect any state of affairs that differs more than incrementally from the status quo whenever one is justified in the belief that this envisioned state of affairs is preferable to the status quo.

The Blinder-View Fallacy

Perhaps the most exasperating fallacy that serves to deflect attempts at sound educational policy making is the blinder-view fallacy. Blinders are used on horses to prevent them from seeing anything that might divert their attention from proceeding directly where they are supposed to be headed. In other words, one puts blinders on a horse when he wants the horse to head for one goal and one goal only. Especially with the recent financial bind in which administrators find their educational institutions, considerable numbers of administrators have chosen to don cost-efficiency blinders so that in making educational policy they can attend carefully to the important task of "stretching the educational dollar." By limiting their vision to a fairly small segment of "normal" cultural vision, these educational policy makers are able to see more clearly and simply what policies must be made if education is to be conducted as cost-efficiently as possible. That is, by restricting their vision to units of production and dollars, they are neither distracted by issues that are not relevant to cost-effectiveness nor tempted to complicate calculations "unnecessarily."

With such a cost-efficiency blinder, policy decisions become almost mathematically neat. For example, one can decide what degree programs should be allowed by counting the number of degrees produced by each production unit and then computing the dollar amount that each production unit requires for the production of each degree. If, for example, not many students elect to take master of arts degrees in the Classics Department, even though enough students may enroll in Greek and Latin to staff the courses that constitute the masters degree programs, the cost-efficiency blinders allow the policy maker to see without distraction that the low ratio of degrees produced to the total instructional dollars spent clearly demonstrates that a master of arts degree in the Classics Department does not give the level of per dollar return that is possible on, say, a Ph.D. degree for which more students opt. From this fact it seems to the be-blindered policy maker that the degree-granting policies of the Department of Classics need to be revised to get rid of the cost-inefficient master of arts degree in classical languages. So as not to appear here to be picking on public officials and school administrators, it should be noted that librarians and teachers also have a favorite set of blinders—blinders that restrict their attention to ease-of-management considerations.

At the core of the blinder-view fallacy is the false statement that if we take into account only one kind of benefits and costs, then the other kinds will remain neutral or "in balance" with respect to the policy means and outcomes. Empirically that is simply not so. The cheapest educational policy is not always the educationally most sound policy. One could identify a fair number of types of benefits and costs that together form our full field of cultural vision, e.g., legal, religious, moral, political, social, psychological, aesthetic, technological, ecological, and others.[10] To put on blinders that would limit our vision to any one or several of these ways of thinking of benefits and costs, to the exclusion of the remaining ways, would be to deny ourselves in our educational policy-making roles access to the full richness and wisdom of our culture. Somehow it seems patently absurd for anyone knowingly to don such blinders for the making of *educational* policy, especially if one of the purposes of education is to initiate persons into the culture.[11]

The Fallacy of Infallible Innovation

If one adjective is presently used more than any other as a term of commendation when referring to educational administrators or teachers, it is "innovative." It connotes far more than being introductive of things new. The baggage of the adjective includes "clever," "realistic," "action-oriented," "creative," "concerned," and perhaps even "right." To be sure, the educational policy maker who has a reputation for being "not at all innovative" is understood to be pretty much of an uncaring, stodgy dullard who would not know enough to make effective policies if he tried. A parent, in a pinch, wouldn't mind sending his child to a "fairly innovative" teacher. And the librarian would likely smirk with delight if characterized as "highly innovative."

[10] For the same point made in other contexts, see David K. Cohen and Michael S. Garet, "Reforming Educational Policy with Applied Social Research," *Harvard Educational Review* 45, no. 1 (February 1975): 42; and Alex C. Michalos, "Rationality Between the Maximizers and Satisficers," *Policy Sciences* 4, no. 2 (June 1973): 242.

[11] For a presentation of this view of education, see R. S. Peters, "Education as Initiation," in his *Authority, Responsibility and Education* (London: George Allen & Unwin, 1973).

Behind the prestigious status of being labeled innovative is the concept of innovation as a change that is necessarily good. Nay, it should be put otherwise: change, for which innovation is a synonym, is necessarily desirable. *Necessarily* desirable. That is, a change of educational policy is by definition necessarily good, which means that the new policy is invariably better than the old. That is what constitutes the fallacy of infallible innovation. An empirical falsehood is mistaken for an analytic truth. One picks up strong scents of the fallacy of infallible innovation especially among the popular critics of public schooling. Not that school critics from Neill to Illich and from Holt to Goodman have nothing sound to say about the status quo. Indeed they do. At times their criticisms have been as astute, insightful, and well founded as *any* criticisms of schooling. But when it comes to providing equally as careful justification for their own proposals as they mustered for their criticisms of schooling, they not uncommonly commit themselves to the fallacy of infallible innovation. This is to say, they slip in a premise (which happens to be necessary to their arguments) which states that any change from an existing bad educational policy would necessarily constitute a good policy.[12]

For our purposes, perhaps the most important point about the fallacy of infallible innovation is that when policy decisions are founded on it, often not even a nod of recognition is given to the empirical claims embedded in those policy choices. The tacit mistaken-as-analytic claim goes as follows: if the present policy is not achieving intended results, a new one will. The effectiveness test (chapter 4) is thus by-passed, for it appears that there is no reason to ask whether X-C is likely to effect S. The answer is al-

---

[12] For a collection of papers that critique numerous such proposals for reform of schooling, see Cornelius J. Troost, ed., *Radical School Reform: Critique and Alternatives* (Boston: Little, Brown, 1973).

ready "known": it will. Here an interlocutor might speak forth: "But so what if the fallacy of infallible innovation detours the policy maker around the effectiveness test? Anyone who has tried to inform their policy decisions with existing empirical research knows well that most likely no researcher has dealt with the policy maker's particular questions and so one ends up guessing anyhow." How should we respond? Yes, basic empirical research often is less informative than we would like it to be, and even when we have access to relevant policy research it may not be usable in policy making because it may identify variables that no policy agent could manipulate.[13] But neither of these points makes the fallacy of the infallible innovation any less fallacious. Merely because it is often difficult, the intelligent thing to do would *not* be to skip the effectiveness test. Sound policy making requires that *at least* we acknowledge the strength of empirical grounds on which we decide to change educational policies.[14] In capsule form, the antidote to the fallacy of infallible innovation is the principle that *the effectiveness test as an empirical test is not give-up-able*.

The Crisis Fallacy

For a picture of a situation in which the crisis fallacy typically comes into play, consider the following scenario. At one of their meetings the school board of the Avant-Garde School District decided to promote the establishment of a district office for the evaluation of teachers. When they

[13] For an especially cogent consideration of how policy research might be made more useful to the policy maker, see Robert A. Scott and Arnold Shore, "Sociology and Policy Analysis," *American Sociologist* 9, no. 2 (1974): 51–59.

[14] For a convenient collection of papers on issues in *educational* policy research, see *Education and Urban Society* 7, no. 3 (May 1975): 211–352.

announced their intent, teachers, students, and the community all enthusiastically endorsed the idea. The teachers had for long thought that the haphazard, uneven way in which the evaluation of teachers had been handled did not give teachers credit where credit was due. The students believed that such an office would weed out the teachers whose teaching they did not like, and in various ways members of the community expressed their delight at the thought of a watchdog agency for tax-paid teachers. With such indisputable support the school board decided to act within the year to set up the specially staffed office. On the evening that they were to decide what sorts of staff expertise they wanted in the Office of Teacher Evaluation (OTE), the crisis question arose: what ought to constitute teacher evaluation?

Viewed by itself, this question does not suggest a crisis, but in the context it had to be treated as a crisis. Any delay or a wrong answer could be devastating. If they were to postpone deciding what should constitute teacher evaluation and proceed directly to setting up the OTE, they might hire a staff that would not have the appropriate knowledge and skills; on the other hand, if they were to postpone the establishment of the OTE to decide the basic question, the school board would be accused of unnecessary delay. Thus, at the outset of this meeting they all acknowledged that they were faced with a crisis. They would have to decide that very evening what ought to constitute teacher evaluation. So without availing themselves of the careful published thought on the topic and without allowing themselves time for reflection, much less time for hearing views of those who would be affected by an OTE, the school board made a "crisis" decision. As thoughtful persons, the board members recognized that it was really too bad that they had to decide such an important policy-relevant question in such a crisis situation. Unfortunately, this would not be the last time that the board would have to handle such a fundamental question on a crisis basis. No one remembered that at the first board meeting in which the idea for an OTE was mentioned, one of the members did raise the question of what should constitute teacher evaluation. In the expeditious conduct of the meeting, that question was acknowledged as most important, but all agreed, "We should cross that bridge when we come to it."

The crisis fallacy rests on a mistaken belief as to when the bridge has been reached. In this scenario the board spent almost a year collecting positive comments from teachers, students, and the community on what a fine idea an OTE was. During that time they perceived themselves as crossing the in-general-what-a-fine-idea bridge. Perhaps because the "hard" questions—the ones that hit at the heart of quality education—are thought of as difficult to discuss, policy makers like to perceive those bridges being as far down the pike as conceivable. But whatever the reason for the delay in addressing such a fundamental question, its source seems to rest with a faulty perception of when the bridge has been reached. If there is an antidote to the crisis fallacy, it would be a constant, nagging reminder that we have already reached the relevant basic-questions bridge whenever we have decided to undertake the making of any educational policy.

The Déjà Vu Fallacy

Common sense might suggest that the longer a person has been making educational policy, the fewer the mistaken beliefs that will flaw his efforts. But such is not necessarily the case, especially because there is one common fallacy to which the "more experienced" policy maker seems particularly prone. Not that this fallacy sets the stage for poorly considered policy decisions; rather, it serves as a crucial premise in a decision to refuse to reconsider earlier policy decisions.

For a typical context and some common effects of the déjà vu fallacy, picture person T who has been teaching high school biology for the last thirty-one years. Yellowed brittle by the passage of time, the edges of his lecture notes flake and flutter to the floor as he shuffles them on his lectern. Some parents of students in T's class recognize the exercises and tests as the very same ones they had in the course from him.[15] In "required plates" and dissections, the course proceeds as it always has, from worm in the first week to frog in the last. And there is always a "quote for the day" on the chalkboard. While many features of T's routines developed unconsciously as habits, T consciously decided what would constitute the biology curriculum, what teaching methods he would employ, and what resources he would use, though he has never even been conscious of the fact that he frequently ignores the questions of non-white students. That is, his curricular, methodological, and resource policies plus a number of unconsciously acquired habits shape education in his classroom, for better or worse. In the last decade T has received invitations to the annual University Workshop on the Teaching of High School Biology, a program sponsored by the departments of biology and teacher education. T has declined every invitation and intends to continue to do so, for he can see from the brochure that they raise those same questions that seem to come up again and again and again. He muses to himself that he was asking those same questions thirty years ago and wonders if progress will ever come to education.

To extend this illustration, one can imagine like-

[15] With this caricature I wish to suggest *neither* that only the older, "more experienced" *nor* that always the older, "more experienced" educational policy makers commit errors which derive from the déjà vu fallacy.

minded legislators, school board members, administrators, and other educational policy makers who, on overhearing the same questions regarding methodology, curriculum, etc., shake their heads at what seems to them to be demonstrated by the recurrence of those same questions: the fact that educators cannot *settle* on what their educational policies ought to be shows that they are incompetent. In such cases, from a sense of déjà vu it is inferred that there is no productive point in raising "those same questions" again. The fallacious premise is that if a question is correctly answered at time t_1, then the correct answer will be the same at time t_2. I find that frequently behind this false belief is a misunderstanding of questions as labels for enduring truths rather than directional signposts. Perhaps both this thoroughly unscientific view of the role of questions and the déjà vu fallacy might be checked if one were to hold in mind the *principle of the perpetual search.* According to this principle, the point of the recurring questions is to remind us to keep on searching for educationally more potent resources, for more effective methodologies, for more just distributions, for more appropriate curricula, and so on. In other words, the principle of the perpetual search requires that we at least consider and reconsider whether our educational policies (no matter how many years they have survived critical reviews) should be revised.

THE INSTITUTIONAL ENVIRONMENT

In the first four chapters of this book we attended to the elements of educational policy and the considerations that are necessary to the justification of any educational policy. But, as was noted at the outset of this chapter, an educational policy maker might understand what an educational policy is, understand how to test an educational policy for justifiability, and have every intent to bring those understandings to bear when making policy and yet come to policy decisions that do not measure up to those understandings. To help the educational policy maker remember to take into account all those questions that sound policy making requires be answered appropriately, we developed a "check list." To alert the educational policy maker to fallacies that commonly spoil attempts at sound policy making, we identified and tagged several such fallacies and proposed "antidotes" that could be used to help the policy maker expunge those fallacies from the beliefs on which he bases policy decisions. Deciding policies in a way that falls short of what we understand to be sound educational policy making can in some cases be attributed to our failure to take particular conceptual and normative issues into account and to our false beliefs. But forgetfulness and fallacies are not the only sources of unsound policy making. A third source is the institutional arrangements and expectations within which educational policies are made. Insofar as educational policy makers can shape the institutional setting within which they carry on their work, it is important in the most practical of senses that they be alert to general features of educational policy-making environments that discourage sound policy making.

A study to determine which particular elements of the institutional environments of educational policy making serve to discourage and which encourage sound policy decisions clearly lies beyond the bounds of this volume. My remarks here are of a different sort. I should like to draw this work to a close with a few general observations regarding prevalent institutional expectations and arrangements which seem to thwart sound educational policy making. Put another way, I intend these comments to be not definitive, but only suggestive of further matters that any educational policy maker or critic must face if he is actually to apply in practice any of the points discussed in this book.

The educational policy maker is commonly subject to "cruel and unusual" expectations. He is expected to produce policies that will do what he has not the resources to do and is criticized for his failure to produce the impossible. No one would think it reasonable to equip a chef with only a can opener and a shelf of canned goods (no seasonings, fresh foods, cooking utensils, or stove) and then to await nutritious, delectable delights. Yet few have recognized the unreasonableness in equipping educators with what amounts to prison compounds and throngs of daytime inmates (persons who generally have no choice in the matter) and then awaiting the production of responsible, cultured, independent members of the larger social order. To ask that educational policy be conducted with the expectation that noble educational goals can be achieved with inadequate and inappropriate resources is to nurture conditions in which vacuous, "stylish" promises are given undue attention while the more sound policy proposals are ignored. Perhaps when we at last admit that the educational potency of nonschooling resources (e.g., commercial advertising and TV's situation comedies) outstrip the potency of schooling's resources, then we shall either (1) increase the resources available to formal educational institutions so that sound educational policies might satisfy lofty goal expectations or (2) deflate our expectations so that sound educational policy proposals might themselves become fashionable. Or, alternatively, perhaps all agencies that play a major role in the development of persons' beliefs, attitudes, skills, dispositions, values, understandings, and tastes (e.g., mass media and all social institutions) ought to be recognized as educational policy-making agencies and held accountable for sound educational policies.

A second institutional arrangement that thwarts sound educational policy making consists in holding educational policy makers accountable for the success or failure of policies rather than for the quality of their policy decisions. Clearly the success of a policy in achieving specified educational goals is a fine thing, but the success itself is not laudable. It is, instead, the policy decisions that are to be (or not to be) commended. Lauding the successful outcome of a policy would make as much sense as commending the arrow of William Tell for halving the apple. Moreover, when policy makers are held accountable for the outcomes of their policies, then the lucky quack appears to have been doing a better job than the unlucky expert. The point is that until we decide to hold educational policy makers accountable for the soundness of their policy decisions rather than for the policy outcomes, we are operating on a confused notion of educational accountability. Contrary to the popular saying, one *can* argue with success, especially if the luck of the draw is mistaken for success. To be sure, policy researchers should give much attention to policy outcomes, as their role is to uncover what seems to work. And policies themselves should be evaluated in part on their outcomes. But policy makers should be preoccupied with making justifiable policy decisions and should be judged on the soundness of those decisions. Because sound attempts can go awry and shoddy tries can succeed, to evaluate any case of policy making on its outcome is both to pervert the notion of accountability and to discourage concern with the grounds for policy decisions.[16] If, instead, educational policy makers were held accountable for the justifiability of their policy

[16] For a collection of thoughtful papers on the uses and abuses of 'accountability' in educational policy making, see *Regaining Educational Leadership: Critical Essays on PBTE/CBTE, Behavioral Objectives and Accountability*, ed. Ralph A. Smith (New York: John Wiley & Sons, 1975).

decisions, then sound educational policy making would be encouraged.

My final point regards what present institutional arrangements require and what they do not require to be submitted "for the record." Most often, when one goes looking for the policies of educational institutions, one finds no more than a statement of who is to do what under what conditions. (Sometimes one finds even less than that when the policy is stated in the passive voice, e.g., "Each child shall be placed according to. . . .") Frequently there is not even a record of the point of the policy. I have yet to see a systematic record of educational policy making, though, I suspect, some would think legislative records serve such a purpose. To my mind this is a most significant point. What has been selected to be kept on record suggests that while we think it important to know what the policy is, we do not think it important to know on what grounds the policy was made. We would surely think it most odd for a writer of mystery stories to publish only the last page where he tells who stole the precious gems or for a researcher to destroy his evidence and publish only his "findings." We should also find it odd that the reasoning which constitutes a policy decision is not systematically recorded for scrutiny. Anything worth doing is worth doing by virtue of reasons for doing it. Educational policies are no exception. If our educational policies are to be deemed worth our time and resources, then we must keep track of the grounds for our educational policy decisions. And, I suspect, if a record of the bases of each educational policy decision were to become a standard expectation, then in the view of policy makers and policy critics the perceived practical value of soundness in policy decisions would be enhanced.

ABOUT THE AUTHOR

DONNA H. KERR received her Ph.D. in philosophy and education from Columbia University in 1973. In the same year, she accepted an appointment to the faculty of the University of Washington, Seattle, where she teaches the philosophy of education and study of educational policy. Her research now centers on the philosophy of education and social and political philosophy.